T0128375

Two Trees in Eden

in

Eden

DON RANDOLPH

WESTBOW
PRESS®
A DIVISION OF THOMAS NELSON
& ZONDERVAN

WestBow Press books may be ordered through booksellers or by contacting:

WestBow Press
A Division of Thomas Nelson & Zondervan
1663 Liberty Drive
Bloomington, IN 47403
www.westbowpress.com
1 (866) 928-1240

Book cover designed by Hester Janisch of Channel View, Texas.

Scripture taken from the King James Version of the Bible.

ISBN: 978-1-9736-7766-6 (sc)
ISBN: 978-1-9736-7767-3 (hc)
ISBN: 978-1-9736-7765-9 (e)

Library of Congress Control Number: 2019916551

Print information available on the last page.

WestBow Press rev. date: 10/18/2019

I want to acknowledge and thank Hester Janisch for her valuable contribution in editing and proofing this Book.

INTRODUCTION

It was a cool evening in Eden. As usual in the evening a bluish colored mist, the Shekinah Glory of God, permeated the atmosphere in the Garden of Eden and the hearts of the First Couple. Adam and Eve were enjoying the peaceful setting in which they were living. The Angels of God rejoiced over the New Creation God had recently formed out of chaos.

Light was a new concept where chaos had ruled the darkness before Creation. The beauty and splendor of Heaven and the Hosts of Heaven were present during those days of Creation and the days immediately following.

There was plenty of time for Adam and Eve to enjoy the life they were now sharing with each other. It was Heaven on Earth. Adam and Eve had everything they needed to sustain them in the Garden of Paradise. There were plenty of delectable and delicious fruit trees in the Garden which provided them with everything they needed to sustain them and keep them alive.

There were various fruit trees in the Garden which God had planted in Eden for the First Couple. All but one of the trees in the Garden of their Delight had been placed there to sustain them and to remind them of their Creator, God. Adam and Eve were forbidden to eat from one of the trees in the midst (middle) of the Garden. That Tree was the Tree of the Knowledge of Good and Evil.

The Tree of Life in the middle of the Garden was to be their main source of food. Yes, there were many other trees in the Garden, and their fruit was to be eaten daily. The fruit which the Tree of Life produced was the fruit which gave Adam and Eve spiritual life. Through the Tree of Life they communicated with and worshipped the giver of Life, God. As long as Adam and Eve were eating the fruit from the Tree of Life---Life sustained them.

On the other hand, Gold told Adam and Eve not to eat of the fruit from the Tree of the Knowledge of Good and Evil or they would SURELY DIE. (Genesis ch.2 vs. 17). The consequence of eating the forbidden fruit would be spiritual death. The fruit on the Tree of the Knowledge of Good and Evil would bring them tragedy and death if they ate of the Tree.

It was almost time for Adam and Eve to spend some time with their Creator in the cool of the evening. Every evening there was a time set aside for Adam and Eve to communicate with and worship the Father. The love of the Father was something the First Couple experienced from the beginning as they walked and talked with God daily. Nothing unpleasant to the eyes or to the hearts of Adam and Eve had ever entered into the Garden at that time.

There was a Serpent God had created who was called the "most subtle beast of the field." (Genesis ch. 3 vs 1). Although he goes by many names, we know him today as Lucifer, or Satan. Adam and Eve were given charge of the Garden, and God instructed them to dress and keep the Garden and to guard it from all intruders who would do them or their garden harm.

As Adam and Eve were preparing to commune with the Father that evening, the Serpent entered into the Garden. The Serpent approached Eve, and began speaking to her in the Garden. He quickly drew her attention away from her plans to communicate with God. Pointing to the Tree which produced the forbidden fruit, Satan said to Eve "YEA, HATH GOD SAID, YE SHALL NOT EAT OF EVERY TREE OF THE GARDEN?" EVE SAID TO THE SERPENT, "WE MAY EAT OF THE FRUIT OF THE TREES OF THE GARDEN: BUT OF THE FRUIT OF THE TREE WHICH IS IN THE MIDST OF THE GARDEN WE SHALL NOT EAT OF IT, NEITHER SHALL WE TOUCH IT, LEST WE DIE." THEN THE SERPENT SAID TO THE WOMAN, "YE

SHALL NOT SURELY DIE, FOR GOD KNOWS THAT IN THE DAY YOU EAT THEREOF, THEN YOUR EYES SHALL BE OPENED AND YE SHALL BE AS GOD'S KNOWING GOOD AND EVIL." Genesis, Chapter 3, Verses 1-5.

Eve looked at the Forbidden Tree and saw that it looked good for food and was pleasing to the eyes. Eve perceived the Fruit on the Tree was able to make one wise. Eve listened to the voice of the Serpent and ate of the Fruit of the Forbidden Tree. After eating the Fruit, Eve handed it to Adam, and he likewise ate the Forbidden Fruit of the Tree.

Through this act of disobedience, all mankind was tragically plummeted into a dark realm that would only bring chaos and destruction to the human soul and psyche of the entire human race. Adam and his descendants would no longer experience the peace and security the Tree of Life produced. Partaking of the fruit of disobedience always leads one toward the Path of death and destruction.

Suddenly, Adam heard a voice in his Garden calling out to him saying, "Adam, Adam where are you?" (Genesis ch. 3 vs. 9). Adam was accustomed to hearing God's voice in Eden in the cool of the day as he anxiously waited to commune with his Creator. However, now he was experiencing many adverse feelings and emotions which he had never before known or felt. Adam did not understand the gravity of what he had done. He was feeling fear, condemnation, torment and hopelessness, just to name a few. Because of all these negative feelings Adam had never before experienced, he hid himself from the Lord.

The beautiful blue mist in the Garden had departed and there was nothing left but turmoil and chaos where peace and serenity had once ruled. Mankind would spend several millennia in the bondage of sin until God Himself would send a solution for their suffering. The Creator, Jesus Christ, would Himself bring salvation to those who would believe and receive Him as Lord and Savior through His sacrifice on the Cross.

The spirit of man can be likened to a garden. From the seeds you plant in your garden (spirit/heart) you will reap a Bountiful Harvest, whether it be good or bad. The spirit must be guarded with all diligence because out of the heart (spirit) the issues of life proceed.

Through the sacrifice of Christ, mankind is able again to eat of the Tree of Life. However, there are still two trees in each person's garden. Unfortunately, many Christians still eat from both trees. God's people are destroyed by their lack of knowledge. The knowledge that comes from partaking of the forbidden fruit can, and will, bring nothing but heartache, sorrow and more temptation. The process of spiritual and physical death began when Adam and Eve took their focus off of the Tree of Life and ate the Forbidden Fruit.

Searching to gain knowledge and wisdom from the Forbidden Tree will always bring about failure. Because it is satanically inspired, the Forbidden Tree only produces fruit which God rejects. Searching for true Knowledge and Understanding which comes only from the Tree of Life will produce a Harvest of Life Everlasting. We must always stay focused on the Tree of Life if we are going to be Fruitful in Christ. Outside of the Tree of Life there is no Everlasting Life, only death and destruction.

TABLE OF CONTENTS

CHAPTER 1

IN THE BEGINNING

IN THE BEGINNING GOD CREATED THE HEAVEN AND THE EARTH. AND THE EARTH WAS WITHOUT FORM, AND VOID; AND DARKNESS WAS UPON THE FACE OF THE DEEP. AND THE SPIRIT OF GOD MOVED UPON THE FACE OF THE WATERS. AND GOD SAID, LET THERE BE LIGHT: AND THERE WAS LIGHT. AND GOD SAW THE LIGHT THAT IT WAS GOOD; AND GOD DIVIDED THE LIGHT FROM THE DARKNESS. AND GOD CALLED THE LIGHT DAY AND THE DARKNESS HE CALLED NIGHT. Genesis, Chapter 1, Verses 1-5.

In the Story of Creation we find many lessons regarding Spiritual Darkness and Spiritual Light. We find the Story of Christ Jesus, who is the Light of the World, and of Darkness which also dwells upon the earth. The whole Story of Creation is an anomaly which can only be understood by those who are dwelling in the Light of Christ. It is not only a Story of Life, but also of Darkness which represents spiritual death upon the earth.

IN THE BEGINNING God hovered over the Darkness and spoke the creative Words, "Let there be Light." (Genesis ch. 1 vs. 3). The earth was void and without form (it was desolate), and darkness permeated the deep (waters). The word "void" speaks of there being nothing but an emptiness or vacuum in the darkness. This is a type and shadow of men without the Light of Christ illuminating their souls. Without Christ, the Light of the World, all men walk in Darkness.

"LET THERE BE LIGHT," was the voice of God speaking to a World engulfed in total darkness. (See Genesis ch. 1 vs. 3). We know that Christ Jesus is the Light of the World. We know that all things were "CREATED BY HIM; AND WITHOUT HIM WAS NOT ANYTHING MADE THAT WAS MADE. IN HIM WAS LIFE AND THE LIFE WAS THE LIGHT OF MEN. AND THE LIGHT SHINETH IN THE DARKNESS AND THE DARKNESS COMPREHENDED (the darkness could not overtake the light or prevent the light from shining) IT NOT. John, Chapter 1, Verses 3-5.

The Life of Christ is the Light of men. You cannot separate the Life of Christ from the Light of Christ. It is the Life of Christ, the Living Word, which causes us to see and understand the Truth. As the Life of Christ resides within us, the Light of Christ shines and illuminates our soul. Because Christ is Life and His Light dwells within us, we can understand the mysteries of God. We understand that without His Light man is lost and doomed to spend eternity in chains of spiritual darkness.

Darkness still permeates the World and the heart of man where the Light of Christ does not shine. Yes, the entire World is full of God's Glory, but most of the World still walks in spiritual darkness. They cannot see the true Light which is only found in Jesus Christ. Spiritual darkness rules and reigns in the deepest chambers of the souls of men who have not experienced and received the LIGHT OF CHRIST.

For trees, light from the sun is the key to life. Where light is absent, there can only be death and decay. In order for trees to grow and bear fruit, light and water must be present. In the same sense, without Spiritual Light (understanding), the heart of mankind is void of Truth and Understanding, and cannot produce any godly spiritual fruit.

LIGHT AND UNDERSTANDING

Light is prophetic of understanding. The Apostle Paul in praying for the Ephesians wrote: THAT THE GOD OF OUR LORD JESUS CHRIST, THE FATHER OF GLORY, MAY GIVE UNTO YOU THE

SPIRIT OF WISDOM AND REVELATION IN THE KNOWLEDGE OF HIM:WITH THE EYES OF YOUR UNDERSTANDING BEING ENLIGHT-ENED; THAT YE MAY KNOW WHAT IS THE HOPE OF HIS CALLING, AND WHAT IS THE RICHES OF THE GLORY OF HIS INHERITANCE IN THE SAINTS; AND WHAT IS THE EXCEEDING GREATNESS OF HIS POWER TO US-WARD THAT BELIEVE, ACCORDING TO THE WORK-ING OF HIS ALMIGHTY POWER. Ephesians, Chapter 1, Verses 17-19.

Without light I cannot see anything. Light gives me the ability to see the things and places around me. Light helps me to maneuver around this planet without walking into things and hurting myself. Light helps me to see dangers that may be in my pathway. Without light, I would be in total darkness and subject to the things and forces which are around me.

In the same sense, without Spiritual Light (Christ), we cannot see and understand things which are spiritual. Without Christ we walk in darkness and cannot understand Spiritual Truths. Without Christ we cannot see the dangers of living in spiritual darkness and the forces of darkness which are scheming against us. Understanding who Christ is and what He has done for us gives us the ability to walk in His Light. His Light shines in the deepest parts of our souls which once was full of darkness and void of Truth and Understanding.

Paul wrote in Colossians, Chapter 1, Verse 9: WE ALSO DO NOT CEASE TO PRAY FOR YOU, AND DESIRE THAT YOU BE-FILLED WITH THE KNOWLEDGE OF HIS WILL IN ALL WISDOM AND SPIRITUAL UNDERSTANDING. Spiritual Understanding is good, however, we need to be filled with the Knowledge of His Will in ALL WISDOM and SPIRITUAL UNDERSTANDING so: THAT YE MIGHT WALK WORTHY OF THE LORD UNTO ALL PLEASING, BE-ING FRUITFUL IN EVERY GOOD WORK, AND INCREASING IN THE KNOWLEDGE OF GOD. Colossians, Chapter 1, Verse 10. Without Spiritual Light I cannot know the Will of God and I am blinded to the Wisdom of God's Truth. It is the Truth we know that sets us free. It is the Light of His Truth which causes us to find our way through this dark and sinful World.

> THIS I SAY THEREFORE, AND TESTIFY IN THE LORD, THAT YE HENCEFORTH WALK NOT AS OTHER GENTILES WALK, IN THE VANITY OF THEIR MIND, HAVING THE UNDERSTANDING DARKNED, BEING ALIENATED FROM THE LIFE OF GOD THROUGH THE IGNORANCE THAT IS IN THEM, BECAUSE OF THE BLINDNESS OF THE BLINDNESS OF THEIR HEART. Ephesians, Chapter 4, Verses 17-18.

If our understanding is darkened, we are alienated from God and our hearts are blinded; and we live our life in vain. Without Spiritual Light men are condemned to a life of darkness and they are bound in chains of spiritual darkness. However, if men know (understand) the Truth, those chains of darkness will not have dominion over them. Spiritual Truth can only be found in the Light of God's Word.

According to Solomon, Wisdom and Understanding are the principle things. Wisdom and Understanding are the most important things we can possess. Christ, who gives us Understanding, also fills us with His Wisdom. He is our Wisdom and He gives us understanding of how we are to live for Him. In Christ we find all the Wisdom, Knowledge and Understanding we need to please God and perform the good works He has called us to accomplish for Him. By faith in the Blood of Jesus and in His name we possess the power to overcome every obstacle the enemy places in our Path.

Through Knowledge, Wisdom, and Understanding we find the treasures which can only be found in Christ Jesus. To find those treasures we must seek for them with all our heart, soul, mind and strength.

IF WE WALK IN THE LIGHT, AS HE IS IN THE LIGHT, WE WILL HAVE FELLOWSHIP WITH ONE ANOTHER, AND THE BLOOD OF JESUS CHRIST HIS SON CLEANSES US FROM ALL SIN. 1 John, Chapter 1, Verse 7. If we walk in the Light of Christ, we will have fellowship with others who are also bearers of His Light. If we are not fellowshipping with others who are bearers of His Light, then our fellowship is being misdirected and misappropriated. If we walk in His Light, His Blood cleanses us from all sin.

AND GOD SAW THE LIGHT, THAT IT WAS GOOD: AND GOD DIVIDED THE LIGHT FROM THE DARKNESS. AND GOD CALLED THE LIGHT DAY, AND THE DARKNESS HE CALLED NIGHT. AND THE EVENING AND THE MORNING WERE THE FIRST DAY. Genesis, Chapter 1, Verses 4-5.

As children of God we are called the "CHILDREN OF THE LIGHT AND CHILDREN OF THE DAY: WE ARE NOT OF THE NIGHT, NOR OF THE DARKNESS." 1 Thessalonians, Chapter 5, Verse 5. Because the Light of Christ dwells within us, we are separated from the Darkness.

People who are not Children of Light have no spiritual understanding, and their minds cannot comprehend the Truth. They possess no Light to guide them through a World bound by Spiritual Darkness. Their hearts are filled with the Darkness of this present World. Their souls are aimlessly wandering toward eternal judgment and punishment unless they hear, believe and receive the Message of the Cross of Christ. In Christ we find all the HIDDEN TREASURES OF an Abundant Life.

GENESIS

One Sunday Morning I was working on a message regarding the Power of the Tongue which I was going to deliver in Maryville, Tennessee. My main scripture verses were in James, Chapter 3. When I came to Verse 6, the scripture read: AND THE TONGUE IS A FIRE, A WORLD OF INIQUITY: SO IS THE TONGUE

AMONG OURMEMBERS, THAT IT DEFILETH THE WHOLE BODY, AND SETTETH ON FIRE THE WHOLE COURSE OF NATURE; AND IT IS SET ON FIRE OF HELL.

After reading this Verse the Lord told me to look up the word "nature" to see what it meant in the Greek. I found that the word "nature" was translated into English from the Greek word "genesis". Upon further study, I found that the word "genesis" means "beginnings". It does not mean just the beginning of mankind, but the BEGINNINGS of mankind. Genesis focuses on the nature of mankind and the changes which took place in man's natural and spiritual makeup in the beginning.

The word "genesis" speaks of the nature of man and the course his nature took in the beginning of Creation. The entire Book of Genesis is about man's nature and the course his nature took from his humble beginnings in the Garden of Eden to the sojourning of Israel in the Land of Egypt.

In the beginning it was the tongue of the Serpent which was the driving force that brought the downfall of mankind in the Garden of Eden. The Serpent spoke to Eve, beguiling her into eating the Forbidden Fruit. After Adam and Eve ate of the Forbidden Fruit, their whole nature was changed from a God-conscience nature to a Sin-conscience nature. They had sinned and come short of the Glory of God, and the unholy seed of self-righteousness was found in them. From that time forward the depravity of sin and self-centeredness proliferated.

EVEN SO THE TONGUE IS A LITTLE MEMBER, AND BOASTETH GREAT THINGS. BEHOLD HOW GREAT A MATTER A LITTLE FIRE KINDLETH! James 3, Verse 5. After disobeying the Commandment of God, we see Adam and Eve using their tongues superstitiously, blaming someone else for their sin. Adam blamed Eve; Eve blamed the Serpent. Apparently Our First Parents had inherited the Seed of Beguilement from the Serpent. The course mankind's nature was on had been diverted onto a deadly disastrous Path.

BUT THE TONGUE CAN NO MAN TAME; IT IS AN UNRULEY EVIL, FULL OF DEADLY POISON. (James ch. 3 vs. 8) The unholy Seed of the Serpent was now part of the "nature" of man. The deadly poisons produced by the Seed of the Serpent had invaded Eden's Paradise. Man had sinned and the course of nature had been hurled toward perdition. Fortunately God had a Plan that would reverse the course of nature in fallen man, and mankind would again find Eden and all its godly treasures. For all who believe in the sacrifice of Christ the way to the Tree of Life has been restored.

CHAPTER 2

IN THE BEGINNING

AND THE LORD GOD PLANTED A GARDEN IN EDEN; AND HE PUT THE MAN WHOM HE HAD FORMED. AND OUT OF THE GROUND MADE THE LORD TO GROW EVERY TREE THAT IS PLEASANT TO THE SIGHT, AND GOOD FOR FOOD; THE TREE OF LIFE ALSO IN THE MIDST OF THE GARDEN, AND THE TREE OF KNOWLEDGE OF GOOD AND EVIL. AND THE LORD GOD TOOK THE MAN, AND PUT HIM INTO THE GARDEN OF EDEN TO DRESS IT AND TO KEEP IT. AND THE LORD GOD COMMANDED THE MAN SAYING, OF EVERY TREE OF THE GARDEN THOU MAYEST EAT FREELY: BUT OF THE TREE OF THE KNOWLEDGE OF GOOD AND EVIL, THOU SHALT NOT EAT OF IT: FOR IN THE DAY THAT THOU EATEST OF IT THOU SHALT SURELY DIE. Genesis, Chapter 2, Verses 8-9 and 15-17.

As we saw in the Story of Creation, there is a dual application for the things which transpired in the Garden of Eden. The Garden of Eden was not just a physical place, but a spiritual place also. We know this because the two trees which were in the Garden were not the typical everyday trees you can find in your back yard. Thus, they represented something more than normal or natural trees. These Two Trees were planted there to represent spiritual truths which pertain to Life and Death.

Prophetically, the ground and earth speaks of the heart (spirit) of mankind. The spirit within us is like a garden. Words, like seeds, are planted in man's garden. The good seed is the Seed of Christ. The corruptible seed is the seed which is sown by the Serpent, Satan. God planted in the ground (spirit) in Eden the two trees we are going to look at in this book.

There were many other trees God planted in the Garden, but the Tree of Life and the Tree of the Knowledge of Good and Evil are the most important ones. They are representations of the two most important forces and issues mankind has to deal with in life.

The Tree of Life, of course, represented "CHRIST." Jesus Christ is the Life, the Truth and the Way. This Tree represented the Truth and the Way as much as it did Life. As long as Adam and Eve were partaking of the Tree of Life things went well with them. They were in fellowship with Life Himself. Adam walked and fellowshipped with God in the cool of the day in the Garden. It was like Heaven on Earth. In reality, it was Heaven on Earth.

The temptation to eat of the Tree of the Knowledge of Good and Evil is an ongoing battle which every person in the World and in the Church faces every day. This tree is rooted in the Kingdom of Darkness, and the King of that Kingdom continues to beguile the hearts of mankind to EAT or partake of the Forbidden Fruit every day.

On the other hand, the Tree of Life is the source of all Spiritual Life, Truth and Understanding. Everything a person needs spiritually is found in the Tree of Life. This Tree is rooted and grounded in the Kingdom of Heaven where God's Light rules and reigns supreme. CHRIST IS THE LIFE, AND THE LIGHT OF MEN.

THE FORBIDDEN FRUIT

The first commandment mankind broke was when Adam and Eve ate of the forbidden fruit in the Garden of Eden. The Tree of the Knowledge of Good and Evil represented the 'LAW OF SIN AND DEATH." God told Adam and Eve that they would surely die if they ate of this Tree. He did not tell them He would put them to death, but that they would die if they ate of the Fruit of the Tree. FOR THE WAGES OF SIN IS DEATH; BUT THE GIFT OF GOD

IS ETERNAL LIFE THROUGH JESUS CHRIST OUR LORD. Romans, Chapter 6, Verse 23.

God told Adam and Eve there would be severe consequences if they ate of the Tree of the Knowledge of Good and Evil. The consequence of Sin is spiritual death. We know Adam and Eve did not die physically the day they ate of the Forbidden Fruit. However, the process of physical and spiritual death did BEGIN on the day they ate the Forbidden Fruit. It was not only the disobedience of Adam and Eve that eventually caused death, but the Fruit of the Tree itself.

In the Bible "trees" can also represent mankind. The seed of the tree is planted in the earth to grow and bring forth fruit. Adam and Eve were planted or placed in the Garden to DRESS AND KEEP IT. The spiritual part of the Garden would have been Adam's place of spiritual servitude. The word "keep" comes from the Hebrew word which means to "guard". It was Adams responsibility to make sure the garden was kept free of anything that would disturb or hinder his relationship with His Father. He was the guardian of His relationship with God, as we all are.

NOW THE SERPENT WAS MORE SUBTLE THAN ANY BEAST OF THE FIELD WHICH THE LORD GOD HAD MADE. AND HE SAID UNTO THE WOMAN, YEAH HATH GOD SAID, YE SHALL NOT EAT OF EVERY TREE OF THE GARDEN? AND THE WOMAN SAID UNTO THE SERPENT, WE MAY EAT OF THE FRUIT OF THE TREES OF THE GARDEN: BUT OF THE FRUIT OF THE TREE WHICH IS IN THE MIDST OF THE GARDEN, GOD HATH SAID YE SHALL NOT EAT OF IT, NEITHER SHALL YE TOUCH IT, LEST YE DIE. AND THE SERPENT SAID UNTO THE WOMAN, YE SHALL NOT SURELY DIE: FOR GOD DOETH KNOW THAT IN THE DAY YE EAT THEREOF, THEN YOUR EYES SHALL BE OPENED, AND YE SHALL BE AS GODS, KNOWING GOOD AND EVIL. AND WHEN THE WOMAN SAW THAT THE TREE WAS GOOD FOR

FOOD, AND THAT IT WAS PLEASANT TO THE EYES, AND A TREE TO BE DESIRED TO MAKE ONE WISE, SHE TOOK OF THE FRUIT THEREOF, AND DID EAT, AND GAVE ALSO UNTO HER HUSBAND: AND HE DID EAT. AND THE EYES OF THEM BOTH WERE OPENED, AND THEY KNEW THEY WERE NAKED; AND THEY SEWED FIG LEAVES TOGETHER, AND MADE THEMSELVES APRONS. Genesis, Chapter 3, Verses 17.

The suggestion to Eve that God may have meant something other than what He said was in her mind a conundrum. In other words, was it just conjecture or was it the truth? After all, she had never tasted of the Forbidden Fruit before, and she really did not know what would happen to her if she ate of the Tree. All she knew was what God told her regarding the Tree. Now the Serpent was giving her more information about the Tree and the Spirit of Beguilement was subtly drawing her focus away from the Tree of Life.

Eve did not realize the danger she was in as the Serpent beguiled her (falsely reasoned with her) and drew her focus toward the Tree of the Knowledge of Good and Evil. After all, she could see that the Tree was good for food, pleasant to the eyes, and one to be desired because of the wisdom it produced. The Spirit of Confusion always works with the Spirit of Witchcraft to confuse and subdue the mind causing it to take its focus off of Truth. Beguilement has the same effect as a mind altering drug. It confuses the mind and dulls the spiritual senses.

Unfortunately, there are always consequences when we listen to the Serpent rather than listen to the voice of God. Eating of the Forbidden Fruit is a bitter pill to swallow. In the belly it becomes tragically detrimental and chaotic to all who eat. Creation was turned into chaos, and darkness eventually became the norm through the disobedience of Adam and Eve.

Yes, the Tree did possess certain qualities that would make one wise, but it was not the same "wisdom" produced by the Tree of Life. The wisdom the forbidden fruit produced was a devilish, sensual wisdom. WHO IS A WISEMAN AND ENDUED WITH KNOWLEDGE AMONG YOU? LET HIM SHOW OUT OF A GOOD CONVERSATION (lifestyle) HIS WORKS WITH MEEKNESS OF WISDOM. BUT IF YOU HAVE BITTER ENVYING AND STRIFE IN YOUR HEARTS, GLORY NOT, AND LIE NOT AGAINST THE TRUTH. THIS WISDOM DESCENDETH NOT FROM ABOVE, BUT IS EARTHLY, SENSUAL AND DEVILISH. James, Chapter 3, Verses 13- 15.

James, Chapter 3, Verse 16, which is the counterpart to John, 3:16, goes on to say: FOR WHERE ENVY AND STRIFE IS, THERE IS CONFUSION AND EVERY EVIL WORK. Did we see confusion in the Garden of Eden? Did we see strife in the Garden of Eden? Did we see every evil work in the Garden of Eden? We can say "yes" to all these questions.

The Serpent was envious of God's new creation God's new creation. CONFUSION arrived in the Garden to bring strife and every evil work because of the Serpent's jealousy. Lucifer was no longer God's covering Cherub. He was no longer God's anointed one. His authority and beauty had been stripped from him. Lucifer and his angels were cast down to earth because of rebellion and sedition. Every evil spirit was unleashed upon all who would follow in the footsteps of the Serpent's rebellion, starting with Adam and Eve.

The Serpent had planted a seed of doubt into the mind of Eve. Eve reasoned within her mind that what the Serpent had told her could be true. SHE ATE OF THE FORBIDDEN FRUIT AND GAVE ALSO TO HER HUSBAND TO EAT. The Serpent's diabolical scheme had worked and mankind was plunged into a new theater of darkness and depravity.

The Forbidden Fruit contained the seeds of all things that would bring torment, destruction, death and dissimulation to the World. A Pandora's Box of Evil was unleashed upon mankind for every generation to come through the SEED OF REBELLION.

FEAR HATH TORMENT

AND THEY HEARD THE VOICE OF THE LORD GOD WALKING IN THE GARDEN IN THE COOL OF THE DAY: AND ADAM AND HIS WIFE HID THEMSELVES FROM THE PRESENCE OF THE LORD GOD AMONGST THE TREES OF THE GARDEN. AND THE LORD CALLED UNTO ADAM, AND SAID UNTO HIM, WHERE ART THOU? AND HE SAID I HEARD THY VOICE IN THE GARDEN AND I WAS AFRAID, BECAUSE I WAS NAKED: AND I HID MYSELF. AND HE SAID, WHO TOLD THEE THAT THOU WAS NAKED? HAST THOU EATEN OF THE TREE, WHEREOF I COMMANED THEE THAT THOU SHOULDEST NOT EAT? AND THE MAN SAID, THE WOMAN WHOM THOU GAVEST TO BE WITH ME, SHE GAVE ME OF THE TREE, AND I DID EAT. AND THE LORD GOD SAID UNTO THE WOMAN, WHAT IS THIS THAT THOU HAST DONE? AND THE WOMAN SAID, THE SERPENT BEGUILED ME, AND I DID EAT. Genesis, Chapter 3, Verses 8-13

Adam and Eve had never before experienced feelings of fear, shame and condemnation. They were accustomed to peace and security sustained through their relationship with God, their Creator.

Adam had hidden himself from the Presence of the Lord. Adam said he was afraid because he was naked. The problem the First Couple had after they sinned was not their nakedness, but now they were cognizant of their nakedness.

They were not aware they were naked before they sinned because they had done nothing wrong. Now they knew that they were naked, but it was not a natural nakedness. The Holy covering, the Presence of God, had departed from them.

This was one of the spiritual lessons they learned as a consequence of their rebellion.

The problem was not that they were naked before one another, but their sin had made them naked and ashamed before God. It was a spiritual nakedness before God which caused them to feel ashamed. They committed Spiritual Adultery when they listened to the voice of the Serpent and partook of the Forbidden Fruit. When they ate the Forbidden Fruit, they sinned against God and now their ability to have open heartfelt fellowship with Him had been lost. Now, for the first time, Adam was experiencing emotions he had never known or felt before. Adam was afraid, and because he was afraid, he hid himself from the only one who could help him.

Adam was experiencing many negative emotions for the first time. He was confused and afraid. He did not understand everything that had transpired. One thing he did know, however, was that there would be consequences for his actions. BECAUSE FEAR HATH TORMENT, HE THAT HATH FEAR IS NOT MADE PERFECT IN LOVE. 1 John, Chapter 4, Verse 18.

In the Greek the word "torment" speaks of pending judgment. Adam knew he had sinned and that judgment would follow. That is why Adam hid himself from the Presence of God. He was afraid of the punishment he knew would come. He was tormented by the fear of being judged.

Adam's first inclination, after being confronted by God, was to try to cast the blame for his sin on his wife, Eve. Eve, in fearing judgment, then tried to cast blame on the Serpent. The best thing they could have done would have been to repent of their sin and ask for forgiveness.

They tried to hide their shame (sin) by sewing fig leaves together to make aprons for themselves. However, Adam was still afraid when he heard the Lord speaking to him in his Garden.

Fear had entered his heart because he had sinned and judgment was imminent. One of the biggest problems in Christendom today is that God's people are searching for natural remedies for their spiritual problems. The Tree of Life, Christ, is the only answer for the sin problem.

UNTO ADAM ALSO AND TO HIS WIFE DID THE LORD GOD MAKE COATS OF SKINS, AND CLOTHED THEM. Genesis, Chapter 3, Verse 21.

Mankind cannot pay the price for his own sin. Only God can remove the stain of sin in the hearts of men. Many Bible Scholars believe the animal skins God clothed the First Couple with came from innocent lambs. Jesus is the Lamb of God slain for the remission of our sins. BEHOLD THE LAMB OF GOD, WHICH TAKETH AWAY THE SIN OF THE WORLD. John, Chapter 1, Verse 29.

WITHOUT THE SHEDDING OF BLOOD THERE IS NO RE-MISSION OF SIN. Hebrews, Chapter 9, Verse 22. The blood of goats, bulls and lambs where just types and shadows of the pure righteous Blood of the true Lamb of God. Christ would one day shed His Blood on Calvary for the remission of sin.

All Religions, outside of Christianity, are Works Based Religions. However, many Churches are preaching a Works Based Gospel. In reality this is not the Gospel at all, but just a form of godliness. In other words, they teach that you can gain the approval of God and forgiveness of sins by your works. Paul warned the Christians at Galatia that they had been BEWITCHED and were reverting back to a "legalistic" form of Religion because they were advocating works rather than faith.

Today many Churches have fallen prey to the lie that works can get them to Heaven. The Blood Jesus shed at Calvary is the only door to Heaven. Christ is the only Truth that sets men free from the bondage of sin and the only Door by which man can enter Heaven.

A Works Based mentality comes from the Tree of the Knowledge of Good and Evil. It is a trap of Satan which many people in the Church have fallen into. They have taken their eyes off of the Tree of Life and have donned a self-centered mentality. When Paul wrote "I CAN DO ALL THINGS THROUGH CHRIST WHICH STRENGTHENS ME", he was affirming that he depended on the Finished Works of Christ for his salvation and not his works. (See Philippians ch. 4 vs. 13).

If we are working to find the approval of God, we are in essence saying that the Sacrifice of Christ at Calvary was not enough. When we are working to find approval from God, we not resting in the fact that ALL THINGS we have need of spiritually was provided at the Cross. There is nothing we can do to gain the approval of God other than having faith and being obedient to His Commandments.

We are guardians and custodians of our own Spiritual Garden. We have been given the task of protecting our hearts from the schemes of the Evil Empire of Darkness and the Serpent who desires to control our life. We are told to "GUARD OUR HEART (spirit) WITH ALL DILIGENCE BECAUSE OUT OF IT FLOW THE FORCES OF LIFE. Eating of the Tree of Life daily assures us we are on the Path of Spiritual Renewal and Restoration.

CHAPTER 3

THE ROOT OF ALL EVIL

ALL EVIL on this earth is rooted in the Tree of the Knowledge of Good and Evil. FOR THE LOVE OF MONEY IS THE ROOT OF ALL EVIL. 1 Timothy, Chapter 6, Verse 10. The actual Greek translation of this Verse of Scripture says: THE LOVE OF MONEY IS THE ROOT OF ALL KINDS OF EVIL.

It was not the love of money that caused Lucifer to be cast out of Heaven. It was his desire to be greater than God. Lucifer set out to establish his throne above the Throne of God. Once a worshipper of God, Lucifer desired to be worshipped as God. This was his first act of Rebellion.

Can we say then that rebellion is the root of all evil? Rebellion is defined as: "the opposition to established authority, government and/or law." There is no greater authority than God. His Government and Laws are established forever. They cannot and will not be overthrown or changed because they are absolute.

Without established authority, there is chaos and lawlessness. These things in themselves are evil and are rooted in the Tree of the Knowledge of Good and Evil. Mankind would eventually become extinct without institutional government.

Rules and Laws are established to protect people and their environment. The Law of Sin and Death is not just a law God one day decided to write down and enforce. This Law is an Eternal Law which has always existed and will exist throughout Eternity. This Law can never be changed or altered in any manner whatsoever.

There are other laws that exist in the Heavenly Realm which supersede natural laws. One of them is the Law of the Spirit of Life. The First Couple were fulfilling this Law in the Garden before they partook of the Forbidden Fruit.

THERE IS THEREFORE NO CONDEMNATION TO THEM WHICH ARE IN CHRIST JESUS (the Tree of Life) WHO WALK NOT AFTER THE FLESH, BUT AFTER THE SPIRIT. FOR THE LAW OF THE SPIRIT OF LIFE IN CHRIST JESUS HATH MADE ME FREE FROM THE LAW OF SIN AND DEATH. Romans, Chapter 8, Verses 1-2. This Law, coupled with the Law of Faith (see Romans ch. 3 vs. 19-31), nullifies and makes void the Law of Sin and Death. If we are not eating from the Tree of Life, we will suffer eternally because of the Law of Sin and Death.

Evil is not just a force, it is a person. Satan is evil personified. Would evil exist without him? I believe it would. Evil is not just a concept. This is proven by the Law of Sin and Death. If there were no such thing as sin, there would be no Law against sin. Satan's power is rooted and grounded in the Tree of the Knowledge of Good and Evil. Without this power, Satan is rendered impotent.

Certain Spiritual Laws are violated when sin occurs. God gave Adam and Eve the responsibility to prevent sin from having dominion in their life. They were to be keepers of God's Holy Commandment to DRESS AND KEEP the garden and to resist any temptation to eat of the Forbidden Fruit. Unfortunately, there was another voice in the Garden of Eden which opposed the Commandment of God to not eat of the Forbidden Fruit. That voice belonged to the MOST SUBTLE BEAST OF THE FIELD.

Adam and Eve had been given dominion over all the works of God's hands, including the fish of the sea, the fowl of the air and the BEASTS OF THE FIELD. Adam was even given the task of naming each of them. See Genesis, Chapter 2, Verses 1719. Adam and Eve were familiar with the Serpent. We know this because Eve called the Beast of the Field by his name, the Serpent. Eve did not call him "a serpent," but "the Serpent." Adam had even given him his name.

BEGUILEMENT

Beguilement, or witchcraft, which basically means the same thing, is the door through which all evil enters into the lives of people. James 3:16 is the counterpart to John 3:16. James says: FOR WHERE ENVY AND STRIFE IS, THERE IS CONFUSION AND EVERY EVIL WORK. John, 3:16 is about Christ saving people. James, 3:16 is about Satan destroying people.

In the Garden of Eden we saw that Eve was beguiled, or deceived, by the Serpent, Satan. Definitions of beguilement are: to deceive, seduce, delude or lead astray. All beguilement is the process by which someone is manipulated by sorcery into fulfilling the wishes or desires of another person or demon spirit. Beguilement and witchcraft are basically the same thing. Beguilement will always lead to sin when someone partakes of its ungodly fruit.

In Galatians, Chapter 5, we see that Witchcraft is one of the works of the flesh. When we think of Witchcraft we usually envision an ugly looking woman with a big wart on her nose, dressed in black attire, riding on a broom. However, Witchcraft is performed every day in the life of most people.

Witches, practicing the Art of Witchcraft, cast spells through what is known as sorcery. Sorcery is defined as: the art of using drugs and/or enchantments to manipulate and control the minds and actions of people. The power behind the Art of Witchcraft comes from the Serpent, Satan. The Spirit of Deception is subtle and can only be recognized by those who have their senses trained to discern right from wrong.

Manipulation is not always performed by actually drugging people for the purpose of control, but is done by a "Spirit of Witchcraft" using deceptive words or speech. Before World War II, the Spirit of Witchcraft was able to manipulate a whole nation, Germany, to fulfill its will and purpose. Satan controlled the mind of a demented man who eventually drew the entire World into international conflict. I am not saying that all Germans were beguiled by this man's words. However, Hitler did control the Military and used the power of Beguilement to manipulate most of the citizens of Germany.

Deceptive words can act like a drug clouding the mind and confusing the spirit. When drugged a person does not have the presence or clarity of mind to make proper and wise decisions. The witch, or person who is performing the act of manipulation, is also under the spell of demon spirits or is linked to the work of the flesh known as "Witchcraft." People all over the World use these tactics on a daily basis to entice people into doing what they desire for them to perform.

The word "Witchcraft" comes from the Greek word "pharmakia." We get our English word "pharmacy" from this word. Pharmakia, also known as sorcery, deals with the use of drugs, spells, and enchantments. These are designed to cloud or manipulate the physical and/or spiritual senses. In other words, "Beguilement" is used to change or control the natural thoughts, ideas, beliefs or dispositions of people.

The objective of Witchcraft is the control or manipulation of an individual or group of individuals. When deception is performed by the Spirit of Witchcraft, the benefit always goes to the practitioner.

People manipulate each other on a daily basis without realizing they are practicing the Art of Witchcraft. Lying to someone is a form of Witchcraft. A person lies to someone to gain advantage or deceive them for selfish or diabolical reasons. Many people are unaware they are performing Acts of Witchcraft when they are lying to others, or trying to entice or persuade someone to do something they want them to do. These actions are rooted in the Tree of the Knowledge of Good and Evil.

Sorcery produces the same effect as much wine as it intoxicates and confuses the thoughts and senses of a person to the extent they have indulged. When addicted to wine or strong drink, people have no power to resist its deadly fruit. This cause and effect is what happens when a person partakes of, and continues to partake of, the Forbidden Fruit of Deception. Strong Drink is a seducer that maliciously dulls the five physical senses and impairs the ability of one to think and act in a sober manner.

SELF-CENTEREDNESS

AND THE SERPENT SAID UNTO THE WOMAN, YE SHALL NOT SURELY DIE: FOR GOD DOTH KNOW THAT IN THE DAY YE EAT THEREOF, THEN YOUR EYES SHALL BE OPENED, AND YE SHALL BE AS GODS, KNOWING GOOD AND EVIL. AND WHEN THE WOMAN SAW THAT THE TREE WAS GOOD FOR FOOD, AND THAT IT WAS PLEASANT TO THE EYES, A TREE TO BE DESIRED TO MAKE ONE WISE SHE TOOK OF THE FRUIT THEREOF, AND DID EAT, AND GAVE ALSO UNTO HER HUSBAND WITH HER; AND HE DID EAT. AND THE EYES OF THEM BOTH WERE OPENED AND THEY KNEW THEY WERE NAKED; AND THEY SEWED FIG LEAVES TOGETHER AND MADE THEMSELVES APRONS. Genesis, Chapter 3, Verses 4-7.

SELF-CENTERDNESS is one of the disastrous consequences of eating from the Tree which produced (produces) the Forbidden Fruit. The deadly fruit of Self-Centeredness proclaims that I, and I alone, can determine what is right and wrong, and good and evil. Self-Centeredness says that "I am my own god and I can declare and decree what I desire for my life."

Self-Centeredness says that I if I have to I can obtain what I want through beguilement and manipulation.

The desire to BE LIKE GOD was the foundational doctrine of the Serpent. God never intended for man to be his own god. This deception has been passed down through the ages. Even now deception permeates the mind-set of those in the New Age Movement, as well as all who desire to rule their own life. There is nothing NEW about New Age doctrines. These Doctrines have always been rooted and grounded in the Tree of the Knowledge of Good and Evil.

When Adam and Eve sinned in Eden, they took their focus off of the Tree of Life. They looked inwardly and saw that they were naked, because the Presence of God had departed from them. They were now focused on their nakedness and knew they needed a covering for their shame. There was strife between them when God confronted them about their sin. They tried to place the blame for their sin on someone other than themselves. Adam blamed Eve. Eve blamed the Serpent. They were both at fault. WHERE ENVY AND STRIFE IS THERE IS CONFUSION AND EVERY EVIL WORK. James, Chapter 3, Verse 16.

Adam and Eve were confused and afraid after eating the Forbidden Fruit. After all, they had never experienced any of the negative emotions which they were now feeling. The Spirit of Confusion works in harmony with the Spirit of Fear to confound and torment the soul through sorcery, divination and condemnation. If they had returned and eaten of the Tree of Life after they had sinned without justification, the results would have been catastrophic.

The Shekinah Glory that covered Adam and Eve in the Garden of Eden had departed and revealed their spiritual nakedness and shame before God. Their only hope for redemption and justification would have to come from God Himself.

Nothing good comes from partaking of the Tree of the Knowledge of Good and Evil. It contains a deadly poison. Even the good part of the Tree has nothing to do with true goodness and righteousness. Eve saw that the Tree was GOOD FOR FOOD AND A TREE TO BE DESIRED THAT WOULD MAKE HER WISE. Unfortunately, the goodness and wisdom the Forbidden Tree produced was worldly, sensuous and devilish. Eating the Forbidden Fruit did not produce the results she was expecting.

Earthly wisdom focuses inwardly and promotes Self-Centeredness. It is prone to beguile others for selfish and diabolical reasons. Earthly wisdom produces its own righteousness and veils itself from the Truth.

SELF-RIGHTEOUSNESS

SELF-RIGHTEOUSNESS results in SELF-CENTEREDNESS. It is one of the most dangerous side effects which comes from partaking of the Forbidden Fruit. Outside of the Tree of Life there is no true righteousness. Righteousness does not come from a self-seeking mindset, but can only be obtained by partaking of the Tree of Life.

Christ Jesus is our Righteousness. When partaking of the Forbidden Fruit, man will always seek to justify his own actions whether they be good or bad. Adam and Eve tried to hide their sins by sewing fig leaves together, but this was the wrong response which only exacerbated the problem. It was a futile attempt to try and cover their sin. Their main problem was not something they could see, but something they could not see.

The true source of Righteousness and Peace can only be found in the Tree of Life. Man cannot justify his own evil actions by another evil reaction. All religions, outside of Christianity, are futile attempts to justify the sins that separate men from the Tree of Life. Justification can only come from the Tree of Life.

According to Jeremiah "the heart (spirit) of man is deceitful above all things and desperately wicked." Carnal man does not possess the righteousness of God, but will always manufacture his own righteousness. Man without Christ is self-centered, self-willed and self-seeking. This is called Self-Righteousness.

CHRIST-CENTEREDNESS

FOR HE HATH MADE HIM TO BE SIN FOR US, WHO KNEW NO SIN, THAT WE MIGHT BE MADE THE RIGHTEOUSNESS OF GOD IN HIM. 2 Corinthians, Chapter 5, Verse 21.

When Christ Jesus rules and reigns in our heart, there is no room for Self-Centeredness or Self-Righteousness. We cannot be righteous if we sit and rule and reign upon the throne of our own heart. Christ Jesus is our Righteousness--without Him, no righteousness can be found in us.

While living in the Garden of Eden, the First parents were tempted by the Serpent to become LIKE GOD, knowing good and evil by partaking of the Forbidden Fruit. Unfortunately for them, this was just a scheme of the Serpent to separate them from the true source of godly wisdom and understanding by leading them down the Corridors of Sin.

To Eve it may have looked like an opportunity to gain a wealth of knowledge, understanding, influence and power which she did not possess. After all, wisdom and understanding can bring riches and wealth which the unlearned and foolish can never possess. However, to find these so called treasures, Eve had to take her focus off of the true riches found only in the Tree of Life.

Christ is the only source of Righteousness and the true wealth it possesses. To be Christ-Centered is to be found without dissimulation. There is nothing hidden in the Truth. This is why Truth, and only Truth, can set one free from the bondage of sin and the source of the beguiling tactics of the Serpent. It is the Righteousness of Christ in us that sets us free and gives us opportunity to serve Him with a pure heart and disciplined mind.

JUSTICE, JUDGMENT AND JUSTIFICATION

All religions outside of the framework of Christianity are works based religions. Man has to produce his own works to be justified and cleansed from his sins. If their good works outweigh their bad works, they think they are justified. However, no peace can be found in other religions because they are looking to themselves or a false god for redemption instead of Christ, who is our Tree of Life.

When Adam and Eve took their focus off of the Tree of Life (Christ) and placed it onto the Forbidden Tree, they left themselves open to temptation. The Tree of Life was all they needed to sustain them. Jesus is the TRUTH, the LIFE and the WAY. In Him we find all the Wisdom and Goodness we need. Partaking of the wisdom and goodness which the Forbidden Tree produced was tantamount to communing with the Serpent.

God is not only a God of Justice, but also a God of Judgment and Justification. Adam sinned and found himself facing the judgment of death. He tried to justify his own actions by blaming someone else for his sin. Eve did the same. These reactions are the result of eating of the Forbidden Fruit.

Because God is a just God, He could not let the sin of disobedience of Adam and Eve go unpunished. THE WAGES OF SIN IS DEATH. (Romans ch. 6 vs 23). Sin demands payment. Sin was conceived through Disobedience; death was the sentence, and judgment would be severe. God is a God of love, but He is also a God of severity. He expects mankind to obey the Laws which produce godly Righteousness and Faith. The breaking of God's

Laws always produce chaos and confusion which will eventually end in spiritual and physical death.

God is the justifier of mankind. We are justified by having faith in Christ Jesus and what He accomplished at the Cross. It is by His faith we become justified. Man's feeble attempts at justification can only lead to condemnation, judgment and death.

Natural man wishes to control his own destiny by making up his own rules and regulations. He justifies his actions by using poor judgment. THE HEART ABOVE ALL THINGS IS DECEITFUL AND DESPERATELY WICKED. (Jeremiah ch.17 vs. 9). A deceitful heart does not use godly judgment because it lacks wisdom.

JUSTICE AND JUDGMENT ARE THE HABITATIONS OF THY THRONE: MERCY AND TRUTH SHALL GO BEFORE THY FACE. Psalms 89, Verse 14. God chooses Justification rather than judgment and condemnation because He Himself is Just. We are justified when we accept the Plan of Salvation which God wrought in Christ Jesus. Judgment is deferred and Justification becomes our seal of approval. Yet, unless we repent we will experience the "severity of God." Jesus paid the penalty at Calvary so justice could be served. He received the punishment we deserved for our sins.

Christ alone is our Justifier. The Faith is the principle by which we who have been justified live. God imparts a Living Faith to all who believe in Jesus. WITHOUT FAITH IT IS IMPOSSIBLE TO PLEASE HIM. Hebrews, Chapter 11, Verse 6.

THE JUST SHALL LIVE BY HIS FAITH. Hebrews, Chapter 10, Verse 38. Faith is a prerequisite for Justification. We must have Faith in the finished works of Christ which He wrought at Calvary.

Without the Living Word, Jesus, prevailing in our hearts, Faith is diminished and we lack Justification. We are justified when we believe and accept Christ and His sacrifice upon the Cross. He even gives us the Faith to receive Justification. Because of the Sacrifice of Christ---where condemnation and judgment impaled---Justice, and Justification Prevailed.

God Himself provided a way for man's justification. Through our faith in the shed Blood of Christ, we have been born into a Kingdom which operates according to the principles of Faith. However, our Faith must be a working Faith. A working Faith not only says, I CAN DO ALL THINGS THROUGH CHRIST WHICH STRENGTHENS ME, but it is a Faith that walks in the reality of that statement. (See Philippians ch. 4 vs. 13).

God is a God of Justification. He did not intend for anyone to come short of His Glory and fall from His Grace. However, He knew from the beginning that man would fail.

Thankfully, He also provided a way for man to be justified by Faith. Man could again partake of the Tree of Life, and Christ alone would have to be the one to bring Justification to man in his fallen state. This plan would be carried out just outside of the City of Jerusalem some 2000 years ago on a Hill called MOUNT CALVARY.

CHAPTER 4

THE SEED OF WRATH

AND ADAM KNEW EVE HIS WIFE; AND SHE CONCEIVED, AND BARE CAIN, AND SAID I HAVE GOTTEN A MAN FROM THE LORD. AND SHE AGAIN BARE HIS BROTHER ABEL. AND ABEL WAS A KEEPER OF SHEEP, BUT CAIN WAS A TILLER OF THE GROUND. AND IN PROCESS OF TIME IT CAME TO PASS, THAT CAIN BROUGHT OF THE FRUIT OF THE GROUND AN OFFERING UNTO THE LORD. AND ABEL, HE ALSO BROUGHT OF THE FIRSTLINGS OF HIS FLOCK AND OF THE FAT THEREOF. AND THE LORD HAD RESPECT UNTO ABEL AND TO HIS OFFERING: BUT UNTO CAIN AND HIS OFFERING HE HAD NOT RESPECT. AND CAIN WAS VERY WROTH, AND HIS COUNTENANCE FELL. AND THE LORD SAID UNTO CAIN, WHY ART THOU WROTH? AND WHY IS THY COUNTENEANCE FALLEN? IF THOU DOEST WELL, SHALL THOU NOT BE ACCEPTED? AND IF THOU DOETH NOT WELL, SIN LIETH AT THE DOOR. AND UNTO THEE SHALL BE HIS DESIRE, AND THOU SHALT RULE OVER HIM. AND CAIN TALKED WITH ABEL HIS BROTHER; AND IT CAME TO PASS, WHEN THEY WERE IN THE FIELD, THAT CAIN ROSE UP AGAINST ABEL HIS BROTHER, AND SLEW HIM. Genesis, Chapter 4, Verses 1-8.

Cain and Abel each brought sacrifices to the Lord, but Cain's sacrifice was not accepted by God. Cain's sacrifice was NOT a sacrifice of faith, but one of works. You could say Cain's sacrifice was rooted and grounded in the Tree of the Knowledge of Good and Evil. It was a work of the flesh.

On the other hand, God was satisfied with Abel's sacrifice because it was an act of faith representing the sacrifice of Christ at Calvary. "Without faith it is impossible to please God." God cannot and will not accept any sacrifice which originates from the Forbidden Tree.

A "Blood Sacrifice" was a prophetic representation of Christ on the Cross pouring out His Blood as an offering for sin. The Blood of Christ was, and continues to be, the only acceptable sacrifice for sin God recognizes.

Cain slew Abel in a jealous rage. The fruit the Tree of the Knowledge of Good and Evil produces is devilish and is easily provoked. It was obvious that the nature of the Serpent had found residence in the heart of Cain. His ideas concerning sacrificial justification were feeble minded and not very well thought out. Abel knew what God expected of him. He proved that by offering the only sacrifice God would accept; a sacrifice based on faith. Cain, on the other hand, brought a sacrifice of his own choosing.

Cain thought he was justified in killing his brother. He made up his own rules, and they had been challenged by an outside source displaying Righteousness, his brother Abel. Cain's sacrifice was of his own choosing and it did not matter to him whether or not it was pleasing to God. Cain was the ruler of his own domain, and whatever he chose to do was right in his own eyes.

Instead of the God like characteristics which Abel possessed, Cain possessed and displayed many of the motives and attitudes of the Serpent, Satan. The seed which produced the characteristics of the Serpent were passed down to Cain through his parents who had eaten the Forbidden Fruit. On the other hand, the characteristics of Christ were passed down to Abel through his parents.

Cain possessed the same prideful characteristics found in Lucifer. Lucifer had been cast out of Heaven for his rebellious behavior toward God. Rage, jealousy, pride, hatred and murder are all part of the Serpent's ungodly character. Cain had inherited those characteristics from the "Subtle Serpent" who had introduced rebellion to his parents.

In Abel we see the Fruit of Righteousness which represented the Tree of Life. In Cain we see the Fruit of unrighteousness which the Forbidden Tree produces. The sacrifice of Cain was not one of faith, but one of works. The Doctrine of Salvation by works can never wash away sin.

In Cain we can see the Spirit of Jealousy which triggered his hatred for his brother. Cain became very angry (wroth) with Abel, because Abel's sacrifice was accepted by God. Finally, the hate and anger Cain had toward Abel needed an outlet. Abel had made Cain angry, and he determined death was the penalty for Abel's offence. Wrath always seeks justification. However, God is our only Justifier and vengeance is His responsibility. When men eat of the Forbidden Fruit, they will always justify themselves by blaming others for their failures and sins.

Cain's wrath turned into judgment, and judgment into satanically inspired justice, Abel's death. Instead of allowing the "Peace of God" to rule in his heart, Cain allowed himself to be overcome by Fruit the Forbidden Tree produced. The works of the flesh are powerful tools the enemy uses to ensnare and entrap men and women who have taken their focus off of the Tree of Life.

Cain was different from Adam, his father. When Adam sinned in the Garden he tried to hide his shame. When confronted by God, Adam tried to justify himself by blaming Eve for his sin. Adam knew he had done wrong and knew that judgment was imminent. He knew that someone would have to pay for his sin, but he hoped that Eve would be the one to pay the penalty. After all, it was Eve who had given him the Fruit to eat.

Cain, on the other hand, tried to justify his actions by proclaiming he was not his brother's keeper. In asking God the question, "Am I my brother's keeper?" Cain was not just trying to hide his sin, but he was saying he was not responsible for what happened to Abel. To Cain, Abel got what he deserved.

Adam knew he had sinned, and he realized he needed justification for his sin. He started making excuses, and playing the BLAME GAME. Adam needed a way of escape from the judgment he knew would come. He knew he could not be justified unless justification came from another source. That is why he and Eve sewed fig leaves in a feeble attempt to hide their nakedness.

In Cain's heart his own self-righteousness was the means of justification. In other words, Cain made up his own rules, and to him, nothing else mattered. Rebellion is always a byproduct of self-righteousness and self-centeredness.

The fact that Adam knew that judgment was imminent and tried to hide his shame tells us that he knew the relationship between him and God must somehow be restored. Adam knew that what he had done came with severe consequences, and he was looking to escape retribution. He not only tried to deceive God as to who was to blame for his sin, he was also deceiving himself by thinking he could blame his sin on someone else.

We can see the character of the Serpent being passed down to Adam and then to Cain. Shame (sin) needed a covering; and if Adam and Cain could find a scapegoat, the blame could be passed on to someone else.

Cain's poor choice of sacrifice was his first mistake. He should have known what God expected him to bring to the altar. Cain and Abel were raised at the same table. In today's world you could say Cain went to the same Church as Abel and listened to the same sermons as Abel. Yet, there was a vast difference in the two of them. That difference had to do with the Trees from which they ate in their spiritual garden. This principle remains the same today. Children raised in the same household can turn out completely opposite from each other.

If Cain did not know what type of sacrifice God expected of him, it was because he was not listening to the voice of God. God had warned him about his anger problem. (see Gen. ch. 4, vs. 6-7) Cain was self-serving and self-centered and self-motivated.

REBELLION

Rebellion is fueled by "pride." Pride is the reason Lucifer was thrown out of Heaven. Cain was not interested in what God wanted or expected of him, but in what HE wanted to give God. He knew God expected a sacrifice, but he, and not God, would choose what sacrifice he would offer.

Cain's sacrifice was not a sacrifice of his reasonable service, but one of his own choosing. It was not only the sacrifice Cain brought to the altar that God rejected, but the motive behind the sacrifice. All have sinned and come short of the glory of God and need justification. Only true repentance can bring Salvation to the heart of mankind.

Abel's sacrifice was one of faith. It was prophetic of the sacrifice which Christ would make on Mount Calvary. Christ was the Unblemished Lamb that came to take away the sins of the World. Cain's sacrifice was one he himself produced by working with his hands. Abel's was a sacrifice of the heart. His focus was on his Redeemer, Christ, the Tree of Life. Cain's sacrifice was a byproduct of the works of his own hands inspired by the Tree of the Knowledge of Good and Evil.

Self-righteousness and Pride drink from the same bitter fountain which came forth when Lucifer desired the Throne of God. Satan had removed God from the throne of his heart. He desired the Throne of God, so he could be worshipped as a god.

THE HEAVEN IS MY THRONE, AND THE EARTH (spirit) IS MY FOOTSTOOL: WHERE IS THE HOUSE THAT YE BUILD UNTO ME? AND WHERE IS THE PLACE OF MY REST. Isaiah, Chapter 66, Verse 1. Self-righteousness rules its own kingdom and does not allow the True God a place of rest. Therefore, there is no rest in the hearts of men without the Righteousness of Christ.

On the Seventh Day of Creation God rested FROM all the WORKS OF HIS HANDS. He had created man, and now His Spirit rested in Adam. In Eden that rest was disturbed by the Serpent, and God's Throne had again been challenged by the sin of Pride. However, this time the Throne of God rested in the heart of His new creation, Adam.

Satan challenges and attacks the Authority of God and His Word whenever and wherever he finds opportunity. His challenge did not work in Heaven. God prevailed--Lucifer was cast down to Earth. Now Satan walks about the Earth like a roaring Lion seeking whom he may devour.

The Seed of Wrath in Cain searched for its own justification. However, wrath in the heart of man can never be justified. God is the only one qualified to administer Wrath. God's Wrath is always justified, and His judgments are a result of His Mercy.

Wrath is an ungodly emotion and is defined as an "unjustified anger accompanied by a strong desire for vengeance." Wrath is anger multiplied many times over. According to Scripture, we can be angry and not sin, however, wrath can never be justified in mankind. Vengeance belongs to the Lord. It is God's responsibility to condemn, judge and/or justify. In reality, we condemn ourselves by our actions. We are justified and/or condemned by our words and actions, and without Christ, man is already condemned.

Wrath is found in the heart of one who has no self-control. Wrath, in natural man, is controlled by the Spirits of Murder and Hatred. Wrath is provoked by the Spirits of Jealousy, Confusion, Strife and Rebellion.

Wrath can control a person when his pride and insecurity are threatened or injured. A wrathful person has a warped sense of justice and always uses very poor judgment. He makes up his own rules and does not adhere to Truth or common sense. Nothing matters to him except his own selfish desires and motives.

Cain was ruled by the nature of the Serpent. His wrath and craving for vengeance was more than any natural man could bear. The only thing that would satisfy Cain was the elimination of his greatest threat, Abel. Cain did not realize his greatest enemy was not Abel, but the Seed Nature of the Serpent which he inherited from his parents.

Eating of the "Forbidden Fruit" tends to cause men to make up their own rules and regulations. Man's rules and regulations will always be of benefit to themselves rather than others. Men without a shred of conscience can be vindictive and will always deal with others acrimoniously. Wrath can mesmerize and beguile the heart of anyone who desires judgment and condemnation of others rather than mercy.

Anger can be justified at times and replaced with mercy, but wrath in the "heart of man" can never be justified.

CHAPTER 5

THE SEED OF IDOLATRY

THERE HATH NO TEMPTATION TAKEN YOU BUT SUCH AS IS COMMON TO MAN; BUT GOD IS FAITHFUL, WHO WILL NOT SUFFER YOU TO BE TEMPTED ABOVE THAT YE ARE ABLE; BUT WILL WITH THE TEMPTATION ALSO MAKE A WAY OF ESCAPE, THAT YE MAY BE ABLE TO BEAR IT. WHEREFORE, MY DEARLY BELOVED, FLEE FROM IDOLA-TRY. 1 Corinthians, Chapter 10, Verses 13-14.

The Apostle Paul is comparing falling into temptation to Idolatry. Idolatry is "placing anything or anyone above God." The Bible says THOU SHALL HAVE NO OTHER GODS BEFORE ME. Exodus, Chapter 20, Verse 3. It is not a sin to be tempted, but it is a sin when men allow themselves to be beguiled and led into Idolatry. God has provided a way of escape from Idolatry. That escape is found in partaking of the Tree of Life. Christ, who is our Life, will always lead us away from temptation into the paths of His Righteousness if we place all our faith, trust and hope in Him.

1 Samuel, Chapter 15, Verse 23 says: STUBBORNESS IS AS INIQUITY AND IDOLATRY. Having things MY WAY OR NO WAY has caused the demise of many great and feeble minded men. A stubborn man is one who rules the expanses of his own heart.

He is the last one to recognize that he is wrong and will stand his ground no matter what evidence is presented to him. You cannot reason with someone who is unwilling to receive good advice and godly counsel.

God created man to serve, worship, and fellowship with Him. Sadly, when the First Couple sinned, they inherited many of the unholy attributes of the Serpent. Among the worst of these unholy attributes is the SEED OF IDOLATRY which lies in wait to deceive the masses.

Idolatry is defined as: "the worship of a natural, spiritual or physical god invented or made by men." That god can be anything made of any natural, physical and/or spiritual entity. Since the beginning of time mankind has created and formed gods from the works of their own hands and bowed down to worship them. In reality, these men are being manipulated by demonic powers and entities which draw them away from the Tree of Life and the TRUE GOD, Christ Jesus.

Idolatry always begins with impure motives and attitudes. In thinking he can create a god by works, man becomes an infidel. Spiritual Infidelity is the same as Spiritual Adultery. Mankind creates what he desires to worship in order to satisfy his desire for acceptance and redemption. He places these idols he creates upon the throne of his heart because he feels a void which must be filled. Christ is the only one that can fill that void.

On the other hand, many men set themselves upon the throne of their own hearts. Like Cain, this legitimizes "self" as the ultimate authority in their life. This is known as PRIDE. All of mankind who are not eating from the Tree of Life are eating the Fruit of Pride which ultimately comes from the Forbidden Tree. The most prominent and deceptive Fruit found on the Tree of the Knowledge of God and Evil is the Fruit of Pride.

Pride is the Fruit of Destruction which has caused, and continues to cause, many men to fall into the trap of the Serpent. The Fruit of Pride is a beguiler which continues to damn the souls of many unsuspecting Idolaters. There is no hope or help for mankind outside of the TREE OF LIFE.

While Moses was meeting with God on Mount Sinai in the Wilderness, the Children of Israel created an idol out of the gold they had brought with them from Egypt. It was formed in the likeness of a Golden Calf. The Golden Calf or Bull God was worshipped by the Egyptians. The Bull God was named "APIS" and was worshipped as their God of Prosperity and Fertility.

In creating and bowing down to worship the Golden Calf the Children of Israel were committing Spiritual Idolatry. They were proclaiming that the Egyptian God of Prosperity and Fertility which they created had delivered them from the bondage of their Taskmasters in Egypt. Now they were trusting the Golden Calf which they had created to lead them out of the Wilderness into a land filled with milk and honey.

Many men today continue to worship the god of prosperity. A prosperous Stock Market is even represented by a Bull. It is called a "Bull Market." Natural man worships the physical, spiritual and natural things which are rooted in the Tree of the Knowledge of Good and Evil. Monetary gain continues to bring spiritual and emotional conflict if it is not used for godly purposes. Many men committed suicide after the Stock Market Crash in 1929 because they were distressed and emotionally broken over their monetary losses.

There is nothing wrong with monetary gain. It has been given as a gift to further God's Kingdom and His plan and purpose here on earth. Feeding the poor, clothing the naked and preaching the Gospel of the Kingdom is tantamount to the Will of God being fulfilled on Earth. God gives men wealth so His covenant, will and purpose may be fulfilled and accomplished here on earth. When His will is accomplished, there will be no more need for men to seek monetary gain.

Idolatry comes in many forms and is often hidden behind many different facades. Only the Light from the Tree of Life can expose all the hidden snares the SEED OF IDOLATRY possesses. All philosophies, false religions and false doctrines are mirrored by the Tree of the Knowledge of Good and Evil. All psychology, psychiatry, man-made theology, rumor and theory is rooted in the Tree of the Knowledge of Good and Evil.

The Tree of Life is the only thing which exists that produces Truth, Spiritual Wisdom and Godly Understanding. Only the Tree of Life can produce Spiritual Life. Man cannot live by natural means alone, but by every Word that proceeds out of the mouth of God. The carnal mind is the enemy of God. Keeping our focus on the Tree of Life, Christ Jesus, will lead us into all Truth and ultimately into LIFE EVERLASTING.

FOR TO BE CARNALLY MINDED IS DEATH; BUT TO BE SPIRITUALLY MINDED IS LIFE AND PEACE. BECAUSE THE CARNAL MIND IS EMNITY AGAINST GOD; FOR IT IS NOT SUBJECT TO THE LAW OF GOD, NEITHER INDEED CAN BE. Romans, Chapter 8, Verses 6-7.

EMOTIONS

Our Emotions consist of our feelings and desires. Our WILL is strongly influenced by our emotions, feelings and desires. Emotions strongly influence us to do the things we do, whether they be good or bad, right or wrong. Our emotions are usually controlled by what we have learned, experienced and assimilated physically, mentally, spiritually and psychologically over the years. We act and react according to what motivates us and by what our strongest desires and feelings dictates to us.

If we are eating from the Forbidden Tree, the Lust of the Flesh, the Lust of the Eye and the Pride of Life all contribute to our behavior in one way or another. On the other hand, through Wisdom, the Tree of Life produces only Christ-like behavior in us.

Many emotions reside within the confines of man's spirit because of the Tree of the Knowledge of Good and Evil. Some of the emotions we exhibit are good and some are bad. Some of the bad or negative emotions are named in Galatians, Chapter

5. They include Fear, Anger, Pride, Jealousy and Hatred, just to name a few.

All of the above named emotions create ungodly responses in us resulting in severe consequences when they are triggered. Negative emotions and responses not only hinder the Spirit of Grace, but they hinder the Spirit of Wisdom and Understanding from producing good Fruit in our life. We have no Peace without true Wisdom. The fruit of Godly Wisdom, which is Righteousness, is sown in peace. James, Chapter 3, Verses 17-18.

True Peace is an Emotion which is derived from the Tree of Life. Our Peace is reliant upon the strength of godly emotions. Love is also an emotion. If we possess the God kind of Love, we will desire to share that Love with others in order that they may also experience His Love.

The Light of Understanding, which comes from the Tree of Life, enables us to see the plight of the sinner and love him with the Love of the Father. Seeing through the Light of God's understanding enables us to share the Love of God with all mankind.

If we are motivated by godly emotions, we can lead others to eat from the Tree of Life. All godly emotions come from the Tree of Life. When we make the Tree of Life our only source of Spiritual Food, godly attitudes and emotions will produce godly character within us.

Everything we do and say is a result of our motives, attitudes and emotions. When we are motivated by God's love, we will seek to perform His will with a passion, surpassing any earthly desire or emotion. Old emotions and mind-sets rooted in the Tree of the Knowledge of Good and Evil must be cast down and replaced by the Fruit which is available on the Tree of Life. The carnal mind is the enemy of God because it is sustained by the Forbidden Fruit.

We need to meet with God every day and read and study the Bible daily, prayerfully seeking Him at every moment. God's Word is Spiritual Food which will produce spiritual nourishment and godly fruit within us. If we are not seeking God and partaking of the Tree of Life daily, we will not recognize the schemes of the Devil as he attempts to beguile us into eating the Forbidden Fruit. We must be "STRONG IN THE LORD AND IN THE POWER OF HIS MIGHT," because we face a daily battle with our enemy, Satan.

CHAPTER 6

TWO MEN IN EDEN

THEN THE LORD GOD FORMED MAN OF THE DUST OF THE GROUND, AND BREATHED INTO HIS NOSTRILS THE BREATH (spirit) OF LIFE; AND MAN BECAME A LIVING SOUL. AND THE LORD GOD PLANTED A GARDEN TOWARD THE EAST, IN EDEN; AND THERE HE PLACED THE MAN WHOM HE HAD FORMED. Genesis, Chapter 2,Verses 7-8.

In the Garden of Eden there were two men who walked together in unity. One man was earthly, the other man Heavenly. One man was a created being, the other man the Creator. One man was known as the First Adam, the other man would come to be known as the Second Adam.

THE FIRST MAN ADAM, WAS MADE A LIVING SOUL; THE LAST ADAM (Christ Jesus) WAS MADE A QUICKENING SPIRIT. 1 Corinthians, Chapter 18, Verse 45.

Both Adams were called the SON OF GOD. Luke, when writing about the linage of Christ, states that the first Adam was the SON OF GOD. Luke, Chapter 3, Verse 38. In His fleshly linage Jesus was a descendant of the first Adam, a Son of God. Yet, spiritually, He has always been the Son of God. As Lord and Savior, the Creator Christ took on the "likeness" of sinful flesh (but not sinful flesh) being a descendant of Adam physically. However Jesus, unlike Adam, did not have the proclivity or predisposition to commit sin because He was God incarnate.

Christ was the Creator who came to reclaim His Creation. Christ was there in the Garden of Eden. He was there in the

Wilderness with Moses and the Children of Israel. He was there in the Garden of Gethsemane, praying to His Father. Jesus hung on a Cross, bled and died because of our sins, was raised from the dead, and returned to Heaven. Now He reigns eternally as Kings of Kings and Lord of Lords.

Speaking of Christ, Paul wrote in Hebrews, Chapter 1, Verses 1-3: GOD WHO AT SUNDRY TIMES AND IN DIVERS MANNERS SPAKE IN TIME PAST UNTO THE FATHERS BY THE PROPHETS, HATH IN THESE LAST DAYS SPOKEN UNTO US BY HIS SON, WHOM HE HATH APPOINTED HEIR OF ALL THINGS, BY WHOM HE MADE THE WORLDS: WHO BEING THE BRIGHTNESS OF HIS GLORY, AND THE EXPRESS IMAGE OF HIS PERSON, AND UPHOLDING ALL THINGS BY THE WORD OF HIS POWER, WHEN HE HAD BY HIMSELF PURGED OUR SINS, SAT DOWN ON THE RIGHT HAND OF THE MAJESTY ON HIGH. ALL THINGS WERE MADE BY HIM; AND WITHOUT HIM WAS NOT ANYTHING MADE THAT WAS MADE. IN HIM WAS LIFE; AND THE LIFE WAS THE LIGHT OF MEN. AND THE LIGHT SHINETH IN DARKNESS; AND THE DARKNESS COMPREHENDED IT NOT. John, Chapter 1, Verses 34.

Jesus was the Creator of all things that were created. He Himself breathed life into the nostrils of Adam. Christ was the Light and Understanding which was there IN THE BEGINNING. He was the Light that separated the day from the night. Jesus gave Adam the ability to understand, reason, and make decisions and gave him authority over all the works of His hands.

Adam was given the authority and responsibility to rule the domain God had created for him. This domain was BOTH a natural and a spiritual ONE. Adam was given the responsibility of protecting his domain from all intruders who might enter to disrupt the peace and tranquility of Eden.

Both Adams lived paralleled lives. The First Adam ate the Forbidden Fruit and was condemned to death. The Second Adam, Christ, died so mankind could be justified. The first Adam became the doorway to everlasting death. The Second Adam became the doorway to Everlasting Life. Where the first Adam failed, the Second Adam prevailed.

God was pleased with all that He had created in the beginning. God loved Adam and met with him daily for a time of fellowship. Eden was Adam's Paradise. The Tree of Life (Christ) in the MIDST OF THE GARDEN sustained Adam spiritually. The other trees in the Garden, except the Forbidden Tree, supplied all the physical food he needed.

We cannot begin to imagine all the beauty and splendor that surrounded Adam and Eve in their godly Paradise. Walking and communing with God every day in a glorious spiritual and natural setting can only be compared to dwelling with Him in Heaven. Today, we still have the option of dwelling and communing with God on a daily basis as we partake of the Tree of Life.

Before eating the Forbidden Fruit, Adam and Eve basked in the Presence of God and walked with Him daily. The Forbidden Fruit changed everything. After Adam and Eve fell from Grace, they dwelt in a realm that was sensuous, dangerous and deadly. Through their one act of disobedience, all mankind was plummeted into a dark realm that would only bring chaos and heartache to all mankind.

Adam and his descendants would not eat from the Tree of Life again until the Second Adam, Jesus, arrived on the scene to pay the price for their sins, and the sins of all mankind. Through the sacrifice of the Second Adam, mankind would again know the Peace and Holy Presence of God which the first Adam had experienced.

Searching for Wisdom, Knowledge and Understanding from the Forbidden Tree will always cause mankind to err. The Fruit found on the Tree of Life is the only source of true Wisdom,

Knowledge and Understanding. Jesus Christ is our Wisdom and the source of all Spiritual Knowledge and Understanding. He is the Light that shines through the darkness to guide men down Paths of Righteousness.

PRIDE

Searching for knowledge and wisdom from the Forbidden Tree will always bring about failure and death because the Tree is rooted and grounded in Pride and Rebellion. The Fruit of the Forbidden Tree is bitter and full of poisons which produce death, destruction, evil and chaos. A good example of the consequences of eating the Forbidden Fruit is Lucifer's fall from Heaven because of his pride and rebellion. PRIDE GOETH BEFORE DESTRUCTION, AND AN HAUGHTY SPIRIT BEFORE A FALL. Proverbs, Chapter 16, Verse 18.

Pride is rooted and grounded in the Tree of the Knowledge of Good and Evil. This deadly Fruit can only produce a HARVEST OF REBELLION. When rebellion is promoted, it can spread as quickly as wildfire. One third of the Angels were enticed by SEEDS OF REBELLION, and were cast out of Heaven along with Lucifer.

On the other hand, the Tree of Life will produce a HARVEST OF LIFE EVERLASTING. The spirit of man is likened unto a garden. Whatever seeds you plant in your spirit will grow and give you a great harvest of righteousness or unrighteousness. If you are not KEEPING AND GUARDING YOUR SPIRIT WITH ALL DILIGENCE, you will not produce a Harvest of righteousness but of unrighteousness.

If we are going to have a HARVEST of RIGHTOUSNESS, we must always stay focused on the TREE OF LIFE. Our own spirit must be GUARDED with all diligence because OUT OF THE HEART (spirit) FLOW THE ISSUES (forces) OF LIFE. Proverbs, Chapter 4, Verse 23.

CHAPTER 7

THE SPIRIT OF CONFUSION

AND THE LORD GOD SAID UNTO THE WOMAN, WHAT IS THIS THAT THOU HAST DONE? AND THE WOMAN SAID, THE SERPENT BEGUILED ME AND I DID EAT. Genesis, Chapter 3, Verse 13.

All sin entered into the World through the Spirit of Witchcraft which beguiles and deceives. To beguile means to deceive through false pretense and treachery. The Serpent was the most SUBTLE BEAST OF THE FIELD. The Serpent possessed the ability to cunningly, craftily and subtly deceive Eve into eating the Forbidden Fruit.

When most people think about the word "witchcraft" they picture an ugly old woman with a wart on her nose, dressed in a long black gown, riding on a broom. There is a real Spirit of Witchcraft which Witches obey and entertain. The Spirit of Witchcraft is the driving force behind their craft of deception.

On a more subtle note, every day many people use the Spirit of Witchcraft to control the lives of others. The enemy is always hiding in the shadows to draw man away from the plans and purposes of God. In his letter to the Galatians, the Apostle Paul described Witchcraft as one of the "works of the flesh."

Several years ago the Lord gave me a message entitled "THE MINISTRY OF WITCHCRAFT." Witchcraft is the most subtle and dangerous work of the flesh because it creates an atmosphere of deception. The word "witchcraft" in the Bible is translated from the Greek word "pharmika." Pharmikia is also known as sorcery. The English word "Pharmacy" is derived from the Greek word "pharmika." It deals with the practice, or craft, of using drugs, spells or medicines to alter or control the thoughts, ideas, beliefs and/or emotional dispositions of individuals.

Certain drugs are used to alter the thought patterns of individuals by confusing their minds and feelings. For instance, a pain killer does not actually kill pain. It just helps one endure the pain by clouding or CONFUSING certain areas of the brain. The brain receives messages from the nerves which tells your brain you are hurting.

Various drugs are used by many people to "get high," to escape reality. Many people cannot cope with reality. Mankind was never meant to bear the burden of guilt and shame which results from eating the Forbidden Fruit.

GETTING HIGH on drugs temporarily enhances emotional feelings and physical abilities by beguiling or deceiving the mind and thought patterns of men. Drugs, like Witchcraft, casts a spell upon the psyche of an individual to CONFUSE and deceive him. This causes him to become somewhat disoriented. IN THE SAME WAY the Spirit of Witchcraft confuses certain areas of the mind to control and deceive that person. Witchcraft controls by deception and manipulation.

The Spirit of Witchcraft uses the process of beguilement to alter the thought patterns of individuals through sorcery and confusion. The Spirit of Witchcraft clouds the psyche with CONFUSION in order to manipulate the soul. Satan--in an effort to control the actions, reactions and emotions of individuals-deceives, beguiles and manipulates his victims.

Eve realized that she had been beguiled by the Serpent, and obviously, she understood what beguilement meant. Unfortunately for Eve it was too late. She had eaten of the Forbidden Fruit and, due to her disobedience, sin had entered into Eden.

If we are not familiar with the ways in which Witchcraft operates, we are candidates for inclusion in its deceptively deadly schemes.

Beguilement and Witchcraft is the door by which all evil finds entrance into the hearts and minds of people. Beguilement has been a force to contend with since the beginning of time. From time to time the hearts and minds of unbelievers are controlled and/or influenced to a certain extent by the Spirit of Witchcraft. Unfortunately, many believers fall prey to the wiles of the Serpent occasionally. The Spirit of Witchcraft and the Spirit of Confusion always work together forming an ungodly alliance to confuse and manipulate unsuspecting individuals.

BEGUILEMENT AND THE SPIRIT OF CONFUSION

FOR WHERE ENVYING AND STRIFE IS, THERE IS CONFUSION AND EVERY EVIL WORK. James, Chapter 3, Verse 16. This Verse of Scripture is the counterpart to John 3:16. What John 3:16 is to the Kingdom of God, James 3:16 is to the Kingdom of Darkness. While John 3:16 reveals the Plan of God for our life, James 3:16 reveals the Plan of the Serpent for our life.

God is the administrator of Light, Love and Life. Satan is the administrator of Darkness, Hatred and Death. God is the embodiment of Spiritual Life in the World. Satan is the embodiment of Spiritual Darkness in the World. There is an ongoing furiously-raging battle in the Realm of the Spirit for the souls of men.

The opposite of peace is not conflict but confusion. All wars, conflicts and schisms are instigated by the Spirit of Confusion. People become confused because the Spirit of Confusion blinds their hearts and minds with instability, insecurity, conflict and fear.

The ability to see into the Spirit Realm is called "Discerning of Spirits." To discern means to "see and/or understand." This Gift of the Spirit has operated in my ministry for many years. It is not called the Gift of Discernment, but the Gift of Discerning of Spirits. Discerning of Spirits includes the seeing of good spirits (angels), as well as evil spirits (devils), as they maneuver in the Realm of the Spirit.

I have seen many Christians operate in what I call the "Gift of Suspicion." This is not a gift at all, but a hindrance to the Body of Christ. Suspicion has caused and continues to cause much trouble in the Body of Christ. All spiritual gifts are given to members in the body of Christ for edification and correction, not accusation and the subjugation of its members.

Several years ago as I was praying in my den I saw what looked to me like several demons running around me in a circle. I asked the Lord, "what is that?" The Lord spoke to me and said "That is A Spirit of Confusion." It was only one demon, but it was running around me so fast that it looked like I was surrounded by several demons. This was my first encounter with a Spirit of Confusion. I rebuked the spirit in the Name of Jesus and it left.

I realized the Lord wanted to teach me something about the Spirit of Confusion. I immediately went into my Study and started doing research in the Old Testament regarding confusion. As I was studying, the Lord spoke to me and told me the Spirit of Confusion and the Spirit of Fear usually work together as a team to perform their evil deeds in order to confuse their victims.

The term "running around in circles" refers to confusion. We have all used the word confusion, but we have not really understood that confusion or running around in circles pertains to conflict or the Spirit of Confusion. Generally, people are running around in circles because they are experiencing conflict or confusion in their mind.

Many societies have differing opinions, philosophies and religions which causes conflict with each other. These conflicts are some of the causes of divisions, wars, and seditions.

A lack of understanding in a person's mind plays a large role in the SCHEME OF DECEPTION. Some animals are known to circle their prey in order to "confuse it" so they will have an advantage over their prey. When their prey is CONFUSED, it does not know in which direction to flee.

The second time I saw a Spirit of Confusion was when I was outside praying in my yard. At that time my wife and I lived on a bluff on Lookout Mountain in Northern Alabama. As I was praying, I glanced up into the sky toward Sand Mountain which was across the Valley from where we lived. I saw a much larger Spirit of Confusion in the distance circling over a large area on Sand Mountain.

I immediately recognized this spirit as a "Spirit of Confusion" because it was running around in a circle over the Mountain. This demon looked just like the demon I had seen in my den except for its size. Because the Spirit of Confusion over Sand Mountain was much larger than the one I had previously seen, I realized its powers of deception and sphere of influence were much greater.

This area of Sand Mountain has been called the "Meth Capitol of the United States" by some authorities. Sand Mountain is also known to be a place where many UFO sightings and extraterrestrial activities have occurred. These sightings and activities are still occurring according to some residents. However, I do not believe it is EXTRA-TERRESTRIAL activity, but demonic activity disguised as extra-terrestrial activity.

The Spirit of Confusion I saw over Sand Mountain was much larger and had more power than the first one I had seen. The sphere of influence which this Spirit controls is much larger.

I immediately started dealing with that Spirit, commanding it to relinquish control over its area of authority. When God shows us an evil work in progress, He expects us to deal with it. I would never try to deal with an evil spirit without the Lord leading me to do so, especially one with this much authority.

The Spirit of Confusion is also known as the "SPIRIT OF BABYLON." The name" Babylon" means "City of Confusion." This World is ruled and dominated by evil spirits (demons) which confuse the mind and promote self-righteousness, self-indulgence, selfishness, pride and many other sins. The Nation of Babylon found in history and its religious ideologies and religions were all types and shadow of the inner workings of the Kingdom of Darkness.

The Spirit of Babylon (confusion) is found in every area of society. Confusion rules the Realm of Darkness in the Earth through spiritual adultery, various acts of sexual perversion, lust and apathy, just to name a few.

In the Garden of Eden it was the act of spiritual adultery which Adam and Eve committed that caused them to be removed from their Heavenly Paradise. The Lord tells us to "COME OUT OF HER (Babylon), MY PEOPLE, THAT YE BE NOT PARTAKERS OF HER SINS, AND THAT YE RECEIVE NOT OF HER PLAGUES." Revelation, Chapter 18, Verse 4. Even though this scripture concerns an end-time prophecy, the command to "COME OUT OF HER" has, is, and always will be relevant to each child of God.

To "COME OUT OF BABYLON" is a command---not an option! When we fail to follow the COMMANDS, or the Commandments of God, we will suffer the consequences. If we do not adhere to the Commandment to "COME OUT OF HER," we will suffer the same plagues as Babylon.

Many Christians at times, even though they are born again, can be deceived and find themselves under the influence of a Spirit of Confusion. This happens when they are drawn away from the plans, purposes and influence of the Holy Spirit.

In many ways the Church of Jesus Christ is under the control of the Spirit of Confusion because they do not understand how God ordained the Church to function. There is not supposed to be divisions, schisms, infighting and accusation amongst the Brethren. Many members fight among each other and many church organizations are divided because of petty jealousies and false doctrines. Wherever envy and strife are found, we will find confusion and "EVERY EVIL WORK."

AND HE SAID UNTO THE WOMAN, YE, HATH GOD SAID, YOU SHALL NOT EAT OF EVERY TREE OF THE GARDEN? AND THE WOMAN SAID UNTO THE SERPENT, WE MAY EAT OF THE FRUIT OF THE TREES OF THE GARDEN: BUT OF THE FRUIT OF THE TREE WHICH IS IN THE MIDST OF THE GARDEN, GOD HAS SAID, YOU SHALL NOT EAT OF IT, NEITHER SHALL YOU TOUCH IT, LEST YOU DIE. AND THE SERPENT SAID UNTO THE WOMAN, YOU SHALL NOT SURLEY DIE: FOR GOD DOEST KNOW THAT IN THE DAY YOU EAT THEREOF, THEN YOUR EYES SHALL BE OPENED, AND YOU SHALL BE AS GODS, KNOWING GOOD AND EVIL. Genesis, Chapter 3, Verses 1-5.

IN THE BEGINNING Satan was envious of God's new creation and the fellowship which God had with Adam and Eve. Satan, because of his jealousy, challenged the Commandment of God NOT TO EAT the Forbidden Fruit. Satan planted a "seed of confusion" in the mind of Eve. The "seed of confusion" had some truth embedded within it, however, the seed was not the entire truth. The seed was cursed because it came from the Tree of the Knowledge of Good and Evil.

The seed the Serpent planted in Eve clouded her mind and confused her thinking. The Serpent was then able to manipulate Eve into partaking of the Forbidden Fruit. "AND SHE GAVE ALSO UNTO HER HUSBAND WITH HER; AND HE DID EAT."

Adam confessed to God he was afraid after eating the Forbidden Fruit. He immediately hid himself from the Presence of God. Fear of judgment will always cause people to hide from the Presence (glory) of God. Adam was not only afraid, but confused as to what had happened to him. Anyone who has experienced such a tragic transformation in their thinking and their entire emotional disposition would be thoroughly confused.

Adam had never before experienced such negative and tragic emotions as he felt after disobeying the Commandment of God. FEAR HATH TORMENT, and there can be no greater torment than knowing harsh judgment is imminent and the fact that you had brought on that judgment by an act of your own disobedience.

Sin always produces a Harvest of Conflict, Fear and Judgment. The Tree of Life will always produce a Harvest of Peace, Faith and Justification.

The Spirit of Babylon has conquered, and continues to conquer, nations and capture the hearts, minds and souls of many great men and women through its powers of deception. The roots of the Forbidden Tree reaches to the lowest parts of Hell. Confusion and fear will condemn all those who fall into its subtle traps.

IN THE BEGINNING when Adam sinned, fear and confusion gripped his heart. Adam experienced fear for the first time in his life because he had disobeyed God and eaten of the Forbidden Fruit. Adam's disobedience brought a whole new plague of negative emotions which he had never known before and did not understand. Adam was experiencing guilt, confusion and fear, just to name a few. He hid himself from the PRESENCE of God because "FEAR OF JUDGMENT" now ruled within his heart where the peace of God once rested.

"FEAR HATH TORMENT," according to the Apostle Paul. (See 1 John ch. 4 vs. 18). Adam was tormented by his emotions because he realized there were serious consequences for his disobedience. The consequence of sin is death, but God gives Eternal Life to all who will repent of their sins and trust in Christ. Unfortunately, Adam and Eve did not repent, they tried to hide their sin and shame by placing fig leafs over their nakedness.

Adam told God he was ashamed because he was naked. Adam did not know exactly what he was dealing with or the way to find that peace he had once known. Fellowship with his Creator had been replaced by something so terrible and unspeakable he could not stand to be in the PRESENCE of God.

He started excusing his own sin by blaming it on someone else. This sounds like what many people still do today. No one wants to be responsible for their own sins so they blame someone else. If Adam had felt any remorse over having sinned, he would have surely repented. Instead he blamed his sin on Eve.

The Bible tells us that GODLY SORROW WORKETH REPENTANCE. 2 Corinthians, Chapter 7, Verse 10. Many people are sorry they get caught doing something wrong, however HEART FELT REPENTANCE is the result of GODLY SORROW. A person portraying Godly Sorrow does not blame someone else for his sins. Apparently, Adam had taken on the attributes of unrighteousness from the Seed of the Serpent.

All the filthiness of sin in mankind which has been, and will be, committed on Earth was transferred from the Seed of the Serpent to Adam and Eve as a result of their disobedience. We find that a Pandora's Box of Evil was opened on Earth as sin found a way into Adam's Garden of Peace. Instead of Peace and Righteousness, Adam's Garden was now filled with fear, confusion, bitterness and strife. WHERE ENVY AND STRIFE IS FOUND, confusion and every evil work will be present.

CHAPTER 8

CONFUSION CONTINUES

Through one act of beguilement, the spirits of Confusion and Fear entered into the World. With these spirits came every evil spirit known and unknown to man. Through beguilement the Serpent became the author of confusion, as well as every evil thought and work which has been conceived in the hearts of mankind since the beginning. Confusion will remain a detriment to the souls of men until the day of Christ's return to judge all of our deeds, whether good or bad.

Throughout the ages men have fallen prey to the Spirit of Confusion and the Babylonian System which it created. However, around two thousand years ago Babylon had a contentious encounter with the Spirit of Grace on a Hill outside of Jerusalem. Grace won, and Babylon lost, thus creating the way for mankind to once again know the Peace of God through the shed Blood of Jesus Christ.

WHY DOST THOU SHOW ME INIQUITY, AND CAUSE ME TO BEHOLD GRIEVANCE? FOR SPOILING AND VIOLENCE ARE BEFORE ME: AND THERE ARE THOSE THAT RAISE UP STRIFE AND CONTENTION. THEREFORE THE LAW IS SLACKENED (disregarded) AND JUDGMENT DOTH NEVER GO FORTH: FOR THE WICKED DOTH COMPASS (surrounds with confusion) ABOUT THE RIGHTEOUS; THEREFORE THERE ARE WRONG JUDGMENTS WHICH PROCEEDETH. Habakkuk, Chapter 1, Verses 3-4.

Confusion causes our judgment to be clouded. Wrong decisions are made when the mind is confused. Man cannot make righteous judgments or decisions without the Counsel of

God, especially those pertaining to spiritual matters. Strife and contention are the result of confusion. Fear will also cause people to make wrong choices. Carnal hearts and minds exacerbate the problems confusion brings in unrepentant men and women.

Habakkuk said that strife and contention caused by confusion impeded God's Laws, good judgment and righteousness from being implemented. He said the righteous were surrounded (encompassed by their enemies) because they lacked the capacity to use proper judgment. (See Habakkak ch. 1 vs. 3).

God's people suffer because they lack Spiritual Understanding and Godly Judgment. People fail because their emotional and spiritual makeup qualifies them for failure. However, we have an advocate in Jesus Christ who has shown us how to cast down ungodly emotions, thoughts and the strongholds which are brought about by the Spirit of Confusion.

Christ, the Prince of Peace, frees us from the contentious Spirit of Confusion. We are free from the Law of Sin and Death because Christ has become our Peace through faith in His redemptive works. If we rely on and trust in God, we possess spiritual understanding which enables us to make the right decisions. Because of the redemptive works of Christ, we possess and use Godly Wisdom and Judgment.

Today many people are spiritually naked before the Lord and have no fear of the consequences sin brings. What many people lack today is a sincere "Fear of the Lord." The Fear of the Lord is the beginning of Wisdom, but Wisdom escapes the ungodly. The ungodly will surely perish if they do not repent of their sins.

Shame in the Bible is a negative emotion which always comes as a result of sin. Adam sinned and hid himself from the Presence of God because he was afraid. Adam was afraid because he was naked and knew he could not stand before God without justification. The Shekinah Glory of God which had covered him in the beginning had departed from his Garden of Peace and Tranquility.

Adam was spiritually naked because he had sinned against God, and God's Glory was no longer a covering for him. Sin always leaves man naked without a covering before God. The Blood drenched garment of Christ's righteousness is the only garment which can wash away our sin and cover our shame (nakedness).

According to the Bible, Adam and Eve were naked before they sinned. They were unashamed because they were not cognizant they were naked. The Glory of God was the only covering they needed. There was nothing wrong with them being naked in the natural before each other because they were husband and wife.

Adam and Eve were clothed spiritually with the Glory or the Presence of God, and their natural nakedness was not a problem. Adam never really understood what it meant to be naked before God because he had never been without the Presence of God's Glory. After Adam sinned and the Glory of God left him, he hid from God because he was fearful of the punishment he realized he would receive for his act of disobedience.

In the same way the Glory of God clothed Adam and Eve before the fall; the second Adam, Jesus, covers us with the Garment of His Precious and Righteous Blood. However, if every area of our soulish realm has not been clothed with that covering of Jesus' Blood, nakedness and shame will be present. This explains why sometimes people have victory in some areas of their life. However, in other areas of their life, victory seems to escape them.

When we are born again by the Spirit of Christ, there are still mind-sets which have to be dealt with and overcome. We need to free ourselves from ALL the thoughts and imaginations which exalt themselves against God's knowledge. All thoughts which do not come into alignment with God's Word are thoughts which must be cast down. We must put on the WHOLE armor of God in order to overcome every scheme and fiery dart of the Devil.

If we have not cast down and disposed of every earthly imagination, reason, philosophy or stronghold, our minds are left exposed to the Spirit of Confusion. The Spirit of Confusion comes to bring contention, strife and every evil work to any area of the mind which has not been spiritually cleansed, renewed and covered by the Blood of Christ.

TREACHERY

Confusion and fear reign in the hearts and minds of men today because they reject the whole Council of God. The Spirit of Confusion enters into the minds of men to deal treacherously with them. Confusion challenges the Word of God in believers today in an effort to entice them into believing and following after false doctrines. Unfortunately, many fall prey to Satan's deception.

Confusion challenges, changes and perverts the Will and Way of God in the minds of men who choose to believe a lie rather than the Truth. Christians who have not been rooted and grounded in God's Word are no match for the deceptive tactics of the Spirit of Confusion.

Jeremiah, Chapter 3, Verse 20 states: SURELY AS A WIFE TREACHEROUSLY DEPARTS FROM HER HUSBAND, SO HAVE YE DEALT TREACHEROUSLY WITH ME, O HOUSE OF ISRAEL, SAITH THE LORD. The disobedience of Adam and Eve in the Garden was comparable to spiritual adultery. Spiritual adultery is a willful act of disobedience against the laws and precepts of God. Adam and Eve chose to play the harlot with the Serpent and ended up committing spiritual adultery. We see the Spirit of Adultery being passed down through the ages to the Nation of Israel, and is even prevalent today in many areas of the Church.

When Israel sinned against God their enemies always triumphed over them in battle. However, when they repented of their sins and turned from their wicked ways, God was always there to bring them victory. God has not changed. HE IS THE SAME YESTERDAY, TODAY AND FOREVER. (Hebrews ch. 13 vs. 8). He still prefers justice over judgment. He is quick to forgive and faithful and just to cleanse men from all unrighteousness when they repent of their sins.

David wrote in Psalms 109, Verses 29-30: "LET MINE ADVERSARIES BE CLOTHED WITH SHAME, AND LET THEM COVER THEMSELVES WITH THEIR OWN CONFUSION, AS WITH A MANTLE. I WILL GREATLY PRAISE THE LORD WITH MY MOUTH, YEA, I WILL PRAISE HIM AMONG THE MULTITUDE."

The enemy comes to strip us of the glorious covering of almighty God's Presence, Grace and Glory. Satan comes to clothe us with shame and confusion. However, repentance and the Sacrifice of Praise unto our God will bring us VICTORY. The Blood of Jesus brings confusion to the enemy of our soul. Satan has no defense or weapon he can use or form against the Blood of Jesus. If the Princes of Darkness would have known the power which existed in the Blood of Jesus, they would never have crucified our Lord. The Blood of Jesus brings confusion and total defeat into the ranks of Satan and his Demons.

"WOE TO THE REBELLIOUS CHILDREN, SAITH THE LORD, THAT TAKE COUNSEL, BUT NOT OF ME, AND THAT COVER WITH A COVERING, BUT NOT OF MY SPIRIT, THAT THEY MAY ADD SIN TO SIN. THAT WALK TO GO DOWN INTO EGYPT (THE WORLD), AND HAVE NOT ASKED AT MY MOUTH; TO STRENGTHEN THEMSELVES IN THE STRENGTH OF PHARAOH (SATAN), AND TO TRUST IN THE

SHADOW OF EGYPT (THE WORLD)! THEREFORE SHALL THE STRENGTH OF PHARAOH (SATAN) BE YOUR SHAME, AND THE TRUST IN THE SHADOW OF EGYPT (THE WORLD) YOUR CONFUSION." Isaiah, Chapter 30, Verses 1-3.

God could not have made things any clearer than He stated in these Scriptures. If we listen to the voice of Serpent and eat of the Forbidden Fruit, we will suffer shame. If we trust in what Satan says, and we believe the lies he conjures up and plants in our minds, we will become confused. The consequence of believing and acting on the Serpent's lies causes us to commit spiritual adultery against our Lord. Beguiling men into committing spiritual adultery is the sole (soul) purpose and mission of the Spirit of Confusion.

In Leviticus, Chapter 20, God called ALL forms of sexual perversion "nakedness and confusion." All sexual perverseness wars against righteous behavior and is instigated by the Spirit of Confusion. I did a study on the word "shame" in the Old Testament; and everywhere I found the word "shame," it was always related to "confusion and sexual perversion."

The Spirit of Confusion wars against the Spirit of Truth, Godly Knowledge, Understanding and Wisdom. Satan knows that Truth transforms the unregenerated heart and sets men free. Many times Israel rejected Godly Counsel and found themselves in bondage by the Spirit of Confusion. Because of their disobedience and rebellion they eventually ended up in Babylonian Captivity.

A person who is confused will miss God's direction and counsel. Confusion always tries to draw men away from the Truth and the purpose and plan of God for their life. All who are not born again by the Spirit of God are under the spell of the Spirit of Confusion.

If we are seeking God daily we will not be easily deceived by Satan. We must diligently spend time prayerfully studying God's Word in order to discern the evil plots and schemes of the Devil.

LOST IN THE WOODS

Several years ago I went hunting in the Catoosa Wildlife Management Area near Crossville, Tennessee. I walked out into the woods to hunt in an area where I had hunted many times before. I had a compass with me, but who checks their Compass when they are going into a familiar area?

After a couple of hours of hunting, I realized my surroundings did not look familiar. I turned around and started walking back in the direction where I thought I had entered the woods that morning. After walking for a long time, I realized I was lost for the first time in my life! I had hunted these woods for years, but always had a good idea of where I was at all times. Finding my way back to where I parked my truck, as far as I thought, would not be a problem. I was wrong.

I turned around and looked in all directions to see if any landmarks looked familiar—they did not! Suddenly, I realized I was lost in the woods. In an effort to find my way out of the woods, I walked around about two hours looking for something which looked familiar. Unfortunately, after walking around for a long time I found myself back at the same spot I was when I realized I was lost. When you are lost in the woods you can become disoriented which causes everything to look the same.

I cannot describe the emotions which started enveloping me. They were emotions of hopelessness, helplessness, confusion and fear. I turned from left to right and right to left looking for something which looked familiar. I was confused and did not know which direction I should go in order to find my way out of the woods. No matter in which direction I looked, everything looked the same.

Over the years I have read stories about people being lost in the woods and found dead of exposure after only a few days. Even seasoned hunters have been found dead within a quarter of a mile from their camps or vehicles because they became disoriented and confused.

For a moment I began to panic, but the Holy Spirit rose up within me. I immediately rebuked the Spirits of Fear and Confusion. I searched for a place to stay in case I had to spend the night in the woods. I found a big rock which I could use as a shelter. With a little food and water, and plenty of ammunition, I knew I could last a few days if no one found me. Spending the night in the woods would not be a very pleasant or warm experience, but I knew I would be safe "at the big rock". The territory I was hunting in was very dangerous because many wild hogs, bears and big cats were known to roam that area of the Mountain.

After walking around a bit longer, I then remembered the Sun was behind me when I walked into the woods that morning. It was late afternoon now, and the Sun had long past its position at high Noon. After praying, the thought came to me that all I had to do to get back to my truck was to walk in the opposite direction of the Sun and keep the Sun at my back. After all, I had the Sun at my back when I went into the woods, which would have been due East. With the Sun going down in the West, if I kept the Sun directly behind me, I would be walking back in the direction of my truck.

To make a long story short, I walked about two miles and found myself at the spot where I had entered into the woods. I had been in the woods most of the day and had probably been lost at least five hours. I hate to admit it, but that was not the last time I got lost in the woods. However, each time I remembered the lesson about the Sun, and had no trouble finding my way out.

Being lost without Christ is like "being lost in the woods" and not knowing in which direction to go. I had the presence of mind to rebuke the Spirits of Fear and Confusion and the feelings of hopelessness and helplessness. People who are not born again do not realize they are lost and wander this Worldly Wilderness without any spiritual direction.

People are born in sin, and spiritual confusion is a way of life for them. They do not realize they are walking around lost in the Wilderness. They do not realize they are living in BABYLO- NIAN CAPTIVITY. Babylon means "CITY OF CONFUSION." All who are not born of the Spirit of God dwell in Spiritual Babylon.

In the same manner, many Christians do not realize Satan has built up Babylonian type strongholds in their minds— which leaves them spiritually confused. They lack spiritual understanding concerning the all the ways of God and the ways of the enemy. They are beguiled by the Serpent as Adam and Eve were beguiled in Eden. However, God has given us every weapon in His arsenal to defeat our enemy, Satan.

We must not reject the Counsel of God. If we do, there are severe consequences we will face. Only the Blood of Jesus can free us from the beguilement of sin and its hellish consequences. Only Jesus can lead us out of the Wilderness into a place of Peace and Safety where the enemy cannot harm us.

Confusion perverts the ways of God, foments Rebellion and brings Judgment upon an unsuspecting soul. Where the Spirit of Confusion operates, every evil work lies in wait to perform the Serpent's evil deeds.

God offers us Truth, Righteousness and Peace. The Spirit of Confusion will separate us from the love and counsel of God if we are not eating daily from the Tree of Life. If we let the Peace (Christ) of God rule in our lives, we will always recognize the enemy when he comes to steal, kill and destroy.

If we desire Peace or Wisdom, all we have to do is ask God for it; however, it is essential that we ask in faith with nothing wavering. First, we must CAST OFF the works of darkness and PUT ON the Light of God's Truth and Understanding so we may defeat Satan.

We must possess the Spirit of Truth to combat the Spirit of Confusion. If I am full of the Spirit of Truth, I will find Peace, because the Spirit of Truth has set me free. If the Truth sets me free, I am free indeed--free to live and walk daily with the Prince of Peace as my Buckler and Shield.

When I was lost in the woods I searched for a landmark which would give me some direction. Without Christ, men have no spiritual direction. There is no hope or peace for mankind because he is lost, and without Christ he is lost in a Spiritual Wilderness. I always carried plenty of food, water and ammunition with me when hunting because I want to be prepared for any emergency I might encounter.

In Heavenly Realms Christ is my food and water. Jesus is the Bread of Life and the Living Water which sustains me as I travel this earthly Wilderness. This can be compared to the Children of Israel in the Wilderness. God fed them, and gave them shelter and water. The Rock I found when I was lost would give me shelter and keep me safe from predators when darkness fell. That rock could be compared to Christ the ROCK OF MY SALVATION. He is an EVER PRESENT HELP IN THE TIME OF NEED in a World filled with Darkness.

With the sun (Son) before me, I entered into the Wilderness to hunt. The light (Christ) of the sun helped me to see. The light gave me the ability to see where I was going. Using the sun

(Son) as my direction, I was able to find my way out of the Wilderness and back to safety. We must always let The Son of God be our direction and our focus. Christ will always lead and guide us in the right direction where we can find Peace and Safety in the Tree of Life.

Our journey through life is like a trip through the Wilderness. Like the Children of Israel, we face many dangers and the schemes and fiery darts of the Devil. Moses, a type of Christ, led the Children of Israel through the Wilderness. Many of them did not want to follow the leadership of Moses and murmured and complained against him. Many of them died in the Wilderness because they failed to believe God would protect them and guide them safely to the PROMISED LAND.

In this life, as Followers of Christ, our destination is Heaven. We must be willing to be obedient and faithful as we follow Christ through this Wilderness into the Promised Land, Heaven.

If I am fully trusting in and following Christ as my Lord, the Spirit of Confusion cannot beguile me. Christ is my Protector, Buckler and Shield in every circumstance of life. When we build our house upon Christ, the Rock of our Salvation, the Gates of Hell cannot and will not prevail against it.

CHAPTER 9

THE SEED OF LIFE

IN HIM WAS LIFE; AND THE LIFE WAS THE LIGHT OF MEN. John, Chapter 1, Verse 4. The Seed of Life is found in the Fruit which the Tree of Life bears. The Tree of Life in the Garden of Eden was representative of Christ Jesus. He was the source of Spiritual Life for the first parents as they dwelt safely and securely in the Paradise of God until the Serpent arrived on the scene to tempt them.

When God created Adam in the Garden of Eden, He breathed into his nostrils the BREATH (spirit) OF LIFE. AND THE LORD GOD FORMED MAN OF THE DUST OF THE GROUND, AND BREATHED INTO HIS NOSTRILS THE BREATH OF LIFE; AND MAN BECAME A LIVING SOUL. Genesis, Chapter 2, Verse 7.

Adam was able to commune with God in the Garden because he possessed the "breath" or "Spirit of God" in the beginning. In partaking daily of the Tree of Life, Adam was communing with God. This Holy Communion was his spiritual food. The Tree of Life produces "Life" and all things which pertain to Life and Godliness. Our spiritual Life consists of more than just Life itself, but all things which make up our Spiritual DNA.

The Spiritual DNA in the Seed of Life includes the Blessings of Righteousness, Joy and Peace. The Seed of Life also contains the Presence of Almighty God who administrates all Godly Fruit by His Spirit. Adam was able to commune with God because God's Spirit dwelt within Him. Mankind cannot commune with God unless God's Spirit resides within his heart.

The Bible tells us that words are "seeds." Jesus, in giving the Parable of the Sower, said: "THE SEED IS THE WORD OF GOD." Jesus is called the "WORD OF LIFE." (Mark ch. 4 vs. 14). He is the Seed that came to "BRUISE THE HEAD OF THE SERPENT." Genesis, Chapter 3, Verse 15. The Word of Life is present in the Seed of Life. IN HIM WAS LIFE; AND THE LIFE WAS THE LIGHT OF MEN. John, Chapter 1, Verse 4.

In the Seed of Life we find Light. Light speaks of understanding. We understand that Jesus is Life and the Light which shines into the darkness. The Light of Christ shines into the deepest part of the soul in order to enlighten the eyes of men's understanding. Without the Seed of Life, we have no spiritual understanding or godly wisdom.

FOR THE LAW OF THE SPIRIT OF LIFE IN CHRIST HATH MADE ME FREE FROM THE LAW OF SIN AND DEATH. Romans, Chapter 8, Verse 2. Without the Spirit of Christ living within us, we have no godly understanding or wisdom. The Spirit of Christ is Omnipotent, Omnipresent and Omniscient by virtue of the Holy Spirit. The Seed of Life within us is omnipotent, omnipresent and omniscient. I am not proposing that we are omnipotent, omniscient or omnipresent. However the Spirit of Christ which dwells within us is all of these.

If we allow Him, Christ will dwell within us richly, in all His glory, majesty and power. When Christ dwells within us we are free from the Law of Sin and Death. Christ will dwell within us in all His fullness so we can commune with Him and find the peace and rest only He can bring into our hearts and minds.

Christ is Omnipresent in me. He goes with me wherever I go. When I get to where I am going, He is already there because He is Omnipresent. Christ is Omniscient in me. He possess all knowledge, wisdom and understanding, and helps me no matter in what situation I find myself. Christ is Omnipotent in me.

He gives me the strength and power to DO ALL THINGS WHICH STRENGTHENS ME.

DOMINION OVER SIN

While teaching a Home Bible Study near Nashville, Tennessee, I was answering questions from the group when a woman spoke out and said: "We have to sin every day." I have heard this lie many times in my life from many different sources, including many Pastors. I immediately explained to her that her statement was not true. A statement like that could only come from the Tree of the Knowledge of Good and Evil.

I explained to her that Jesus died on the Cross so that we could have POWER OVER sin, not so sin could prevail over us. Jesus died on the Cross to give us Dominion over sin so that sin could not have Dominion over our life. Her statement and misplaced belief made the POWER OF THE CROSS of no effect in her own life.

This doctrine she had fallen into proclaims that "I must, or will sin every day" is rooted and grounded in the Tree of the Knowledge of Good and Evil. This is a damnable doctrine that leads many down the Path of Perdition.

If I thought that I was required to sin every day, I would not want to get out of bed in the morning, knowing ahead of time that I was going to have to grieve my Lord by having to sin. When I was a sinner, I could not help but sin. I did not have the power within me to stop sinning. Now, however, sin has no more dominion over me. I have been set free from the Law of Sin and Death through the Power of the Risen Christ who dwells within me.

I am not saying I never sin and come short of the Glory of God. However, if, and when I do sin, I have an advocate with the Father who forgives me of my sins and cleanses me from all unrighteousness. I am no longer under the Curse of the Law, but Christ in me is the Hope of my salvation and the one who gives me POWER OVER sin.

WHERE SHALL I GO FROM THY SPIRIT? OR WHERE SHALL I FLEE FROM THY PRESENCE? IF I ASCEND UP TO HEAVEN, THOU ART THERE. IF I MAKE MY BED IN HELL, BEHOLD, THOU ART THERE. IF I TAKE THE WINGS OF THE MORN-ING, AND DWELL IN THE UTTERMOST PARTS OF THE SEA: EVEN THERE SHALL THY HAND LEAD ME, AND THY RIGHT HAND HOLD ME UP. Psalms, 139, Verses 7-10.

The word "spirit" means wind or breath. God can be, and is, everywhere at the same time by His Spirit (Holy Spirit). God is not just a wind or breath, but He is a person with all the knowl-edge, wisdom, understanding and emotions of the Godhead. In Spirit form, God is like a wind or breath.

Jesus said: "THE WORDS (seeds) THAT I SPEAK UNTO YOU, THEY ARE SPIRIT, AND THEY ARE LIFE." John, Chapter 6, Verse 63. In the person of Christ we find the Seed of Salvation through the words He has spoken and the words He continues to speak.

God speaks to us in many different ways. His spoken Word always comes by way of the Spirit of Christ Jesus. The Tes-timony of Christ is the Spirit of Prophecy. These words contain the Seed of Eternal Life. The words of Eternal Life contain within them everything that the message of the Cross and Life itself embodies.

When God created Adam He breathed into Him the "breath (Spirit) of Life" and Adam became a living soul. Genesis, Chapter 2, Verse 7. Since the fall of Adam and the subsequent dispossession of the Spirit of God in mankind, the Redemption of Mankind was needed. Christ, who is our Life, has redeemed us from Sin and the Curse of the Law when we accept Christ as our Lord and Savior. God comes again to dwell in man by His Spirit.

AND IF CHRIST BE IN YOU, THE BODY IS DEAD BECAUSE OF SIN; BUT THE SPIRIT IS LIFE BECAUSE OF RIGHTEOUS-NESS. BUT IF THE SPIRIT OF HIM THAT RAISED UP JESUS FROM THE DEAD DWELLS IN YOU, HE THAT RAISED UP CHRIST JESUS FROM THE DEAD SHALL ALSO QUICKEN YOUR MORTAL BODIES BY HIS SPIRIT THAT DWELLETH IN YOU. Roman, Chapter 8, Verses 1011.

In Christ Jesus we have access to the very nature and power of God because the Spirit of Christ has raised us up to "SIT IN HEAVENLY PLACES WITH HIM." We have "COME UNTO MOUNT ZION, AND UNTO THE HOLY CITY OF THE LIVING GOD, THE HEAV-ENLY JERUSALEM, AND TO AN INNUMERABLE COMPANY OF AN-GELS." Hebrews, Chapter 12, Verses 22.

In Christ was Life and that Life was the Light of men. That Life has enabled us to become the sons and daughters of God. The word "life" comes from the Greek word "Zoe," which speaks of the same Spirit of Life which God possesses. Zoe speaks of Life in the absolute sense, the God kind of Life. The Bible tells us that God is Life. He is not just the creator of life, but He is Zoe Life. In Him, and Him only, we find Life Everlasting.

In Christ that Life (Spirit of Life) is the Light which shines through the darkness and draws men to pursue a renewed rela-tionship with Him. His Light in us reflects the Life of God to a lost and dying world. Light gives understanding. The Light of Christ shines in darkness and cannot be overtaken by the darkness.

Light cannot be overwhelmed by the Forces of Darkness because Light is more powerful than Darkness. If I open my win-dow shades at night, darkness does not come in my house, but light will shine out into the darkness. This is a true representation of the "true Light" which is found only in Jesus Christ. He is the only Light which can be found in this World of Darkness.

The words Jesus speaks to us are "Spirit" and "Life." That Life is the Light which draws men unto Him so He can give to them Spiritual Understanding and Salvation for their souls. Words of Life are words of Light which open the eyes of our understanding as we seek Truth and godly wisdom from Christ on a daily basis.

The Life of God is a never ending cycle. Without Zoe Life, men cannot enter into the Gates of Heaven. Without Zoe, no Eternal Life exists anywhere. Zoe cannot be found, nor will it ever be found, in the confines of evil men or in their motives and attitudes. Without Zoe Life, no one can experience the Light and Life of Christ.

Zoe Life produces and sustains the Life of God which dwells within us. In Christ we find Zoe, which is the more ABUNDANT LIFE. Without Zoe Life, man is destined to spend eternity in everlasting darkness and damnation.

If we are born again by the Spirit of Christ we have become the sons and daughters of Life, and His Light will shine within us throughout Eternity. When we accept Christ and give our life to Him, we become the CHILDREN OF THE DAY; and the Light of His Manifest Presence will guide us through this World of turmoil and darkness

CHAPTER 10

THE SPIRIT OF FEAR

FOR GOD HAS NOT GIVEN US A SPIRIT OF FEAR, BUT OF POWER AND LOVE, AND A SOUND (or disciplined) MIND. Second Timothy, Chapter 1, Verse 7.

The Spirit of Fear was introduced to the World by Satan in the Garden of Eden. Adam sinned, and when he heard God's voice in the Garden he hid himself from the Presence of God because HE WAS AFRAID.

We saw in Chapter 7 how the Spirit of Confusion and the Spirit of Fear often times work together to defeat the plan and purpose of God in our life. The Spirit of Fear is one of the strongest of all evil spirits, as well as one of mankind's greatest enemies. The Spirit of Fear comes in many different forms, shapes and sizes. Fear always carries a suitcase packed with doubt when it visits our hearts and homes.

Fear is accompanied by its companion, Torment. We deny God's Power and His ability to work in our life if we fear. Fear also hinders the Spirit of God's love, faith and compassion from working in and through us. When we fear, a sound (disciplined) mind is not present within us. True Christians stand firm during the enemy's attacks because they possess power, love and a disciplined mind through Christ our Redeemer.

Fear is the opposite of Faith. To a certain extent, all evil spirits have the power to produce fear in the lives of people. However, not all demons carry the rank of "Spirit of Fear." The Spirit of Fear joins together with other spirits in order to perform its unholy missions.

Most people, even Christians, are subject to fear of one kind or another. Fear is a Spirit which can be passed down from generation to generation through generational curses. Many curses, and the propensity to commit certain sins, are passed down to offspring because of the sins of previous generations. If a parent has a Spirit of Fear, there is a good possibility that one, or all of their offspring will also possess that same spirit.

According to the Apostle Paul, "fear has torment." Without faith (the opposite of fear) in God, fear can destroy a person's life, home, family, and all he or she holds dear. While Faith is a unifier, fear is a divider. Without Faith we cannot please God. Without faith we are destined to be controlled and/or tormented by the Spirit of Fear in one way or another.

I cannot communicate in one chapter all the Bible tells us regarding fear, but I can share with you much of what I know and have experienced in dealing with this Spirit. The basic thing we need to understand and know is that this Spirit is evil, and God, through the Blood of Jesus, has given us power to overcome this enemy of our soul.

Many people have fears, and are reluctant or embarrassed to let others know they are fearful because they are afraid (fear) they will be judged for being weak or cowardly. Thus, they languish in their fears and are tormented throughout their entire life.

A Spirit of Violence can cause fear and intimidation when it shows up to create havoc and chaos in the lives of people. A Spirit of Poverty often travels with the Spirit of Fear in order to cause someone to question whether they will have anything to eat, or enough money to pay their bills. A Spirit of fear can grip a person's heart when the Doctor tells them they have a terminal disease. Fear is a Tormentor.

Often the Spirit of Fear will place thoughts in our minds regarding a tragedy of some kind happening to our love ones. Many times the Spirit of Fear places thoughts in our minds of dying or our children or love ones dying. The Spirit of Fear works in the life of people in many different ways. However, we do HAVE AUTHORITY through the "Blood of Christ" to send Satan packing when he or his demons show up on our doorstep with his Weapon of Fear.

INTIMIDATION

Intimidation is another type of Fear. People are intimidated by many things. Thoughts which the enemy sows in the psyche, such as hopelessness, helplessness and depravity are planted there for the purpose of intimidation. It is imperative to remember these thoughts if not cast down will become strongholds in our minds. Thoughts which exalt themselves against the Knowledge of God must be cast down if we are going to live in peace and harmony with God.

Intimidating spirits are more subtle than most of the FEAR-BEARING spirits. Intimidating spirits may suggest to you that you are weak and timid. However, these Spirits need and call upon their stronger compatriots to help them establish greater strongholds of fear and terror in your life.

If we have Faith in Christ, our Intermediary, intimidating spirits cannot build strongholds in our minds. If we have faith in Christ, His power will deliver us from all the strategies of Satan. We must be able to recognize the Spirit of Fear or we will be helpless to render it ineffective. Intimidation cannot get past the Blood of Jesus if we have the Shield of His Faith protecting our hearts and minds.

It is very important for Christians to maintain a clear, clean and blood-washed conscience. Without a clear conscience, we will not be able to defend the territory of our mind and spirit from the wiles and schemes of the Devil. If we are to dwell in the perfect peace which Christ has promised to us, then we must possess the Wisdom He has given us to defeat this enemy which opposes our soul.

THOU WILT KEEP HIM IN PERFECT PEACE, WHOSE MIND IS STAYED ON THEE: BECAUSE HE TRUSTETH IN THEE. Isaiah, Chapter 26, verse 3.

If our peace is going to be perfect, we must strengthen the perimeters of our soul with the parameters of faith and justice through the Blood of Christ. What we sow is what we will reap. The principles, doctrines or philosophies we espouse or build our foundation upon will determine the outcome of our level of peace. We must refrain from all unrighteous behavior if we are going to continue in our quest for that peace which surpasses all human knowledge and understanding.

If we are going to dwell in peace, we must renounce and cast down all man-made principles, doctrines and philosophies. These are all rooted and grounded in the Tree of the Knowledge of Good and Evil.

If we are going to be at peace, we must build strong defenses to overcome fear and intimidation when the enemy strikes. God has not given us a Spirit of Fear, but of "Peace." If we are going to dwell in peace, the Strongholds of Fear must be defeated. GOD HAS NOT GIVEN US A SPIRIT OF FEAR, BUT OF POWER, AND LOVE AND A SOUND MIND. If we fear we have not been made complete in His love.

FEAR OF THE UNKOWN

All fear has to do with something in the future. We do not fear things in the past because the past is history. We do not have to face what has already happened, but what may or will happen in the future. For example, if someone has a fear of water, they will try to stay away from bodies of water. If someone has a fear of elevators, they will walk fifty flights of stairs rather than get on an elevator. These types of fears are more subtle than others.

Sometimes people can sidestep and find a way around fear if they try. Although some fear can usually be sidestepped, people who fear certain things may someday be forced to face and defeat those fears or find themselves tormented by fear.

Many people fear death because they are uncertain of what lies beyond the veil of death. It is not necessarily the pain of death that worries people, but the thoughts of what will happen after they die. Will death be unpleasant, or even unbearable, for them? Will they even exist after death? Will they be at peace or in a place of torment? Is there really a God who lives in a wonderful place called Heaven? Is there really a place called Hell where people are tormented for eternity? What will happen to me when I die?

The fear of death should not enter into a Christian's mind. Heaven is a place where fear does not exist. If we believe in God we should never fear what is beyond the veil of death.

FEAR ALWAYS HAS TO DO WITH THE FUTURE. If we are secure in our relationship with Christ, we will not fear death or any weapon the enemy tries to use against us.

Fear can grip a person's heart when the Doctor tells them they have only a short time to live. Those words can resound over and over in the mind and torment an individual. In fear the person goes and repeats those words to others without getting a second opinion or seeking the counsel of God. We are justified or condemned by the words we speak.

When someone tells me something negative, I always go to the final authority on everything. Jesus is the ultimate authority. Nobody's opinion matters but His. If we allow fear to rule our life it will adversely affect and transmutate our future. Jesus is our Peace even in adverse circumstances.

On the other hand, peace is something which deals with the present. The opposite of peace is conflict, or confusion. If we are not experiencing peace, there is a war going on within our hearts and minds. Christ can keep us in PERFECT PEACE because He is our Peace. Christ will remove the thoughts which bring conflict to the soul, when we are trusting in Him.

Even though we may be at war with the unseen forces of darkness, we can still be at peace in our heart and mind because the Prince of Peace rules and reigns within us. Without that peace, sooner or later the enemy will gain a foothold in our life.

There are many Christians who not only fear the Devil, but they also fear the Spirit of Fear. (See Proverbs, Chapter 3, Verse 25) It is one thing to be afraid of the Devil, but the fear of fear brings even more torment. The consequences of fear is torment—torment is a precursor of judgment.

God is a just God and recompenses evil with harsh judgment. We do not want to find ourselves on the wrong end of His justice and judgment. We are justified through the Blood of Christ. Torment, which fear releases, has no place in the heart of the believer.

If you are ever in the presence of complete unadulterated evil, the Spirit of Fear, you would surely recognize immediately that fear is accompanied by torment. Without faith, which is the opposite of fear, one cannot escape the grasp of fear or its torment.

I have discerned the Spirit of Fear many times in my ministry. Some spirits of fear are larger and more powerful than others. Each and every Spirit of Fear has the power to bring torment. If a person entertains or possesses a Spirit of Fear, that Spirit will torment them.

I have cast the Spirit of Fear out of many Christian people, and in my own life as well, through the power of the Holy Spirit and faith in the finished works of Christ. If the Spirit of Fear is not dealt with appropriately, it will continue to torment a person.

"THE FEARFULL, AND UNBELIEVING AND THE ABOMINABLE, AND MURDERERS, AND WHOREMONGERS, AND SORCERERS, AND IDOLITARS, AND ALL LIARS, SHALL HAVE THEIR PART IN THE LAKE WHICH BURNETH WITH FIRE AND BRIMSTONE; WHICH IS THE SECOND DEATH." Revelation, Chapter 21, Verse 8.

One night after I went to bed a large spirit came into my bedroom. It walked through the open bedroom door and came and stood beside the bed next to me. I immediately sensed an overwhelming presence of fear as it walked up to my bedside. I had seen and discerned many evil spirits in my life, but this was one of the most hideous looking evil spirits I had ever seen.

This Spirit of Fear stood around six feet tall. It had a body like a man. That, in itself, is no big deal because many evil spirits have human-like bodies and many have animal-like bodies. It was the head and face of this spirit which made this devil so hideous looking.

This devil possessed no facial features. This Spirit of Fear had no eyes in order to see. He had no mouth or nose. Fear had no ears, eyes, nose, mouth or any other type of features on his face or head. He could not see to walk because he had no eyes, yet he walked through the doorway and directly to my bedside and stood next to me.

The presence of evil which I saw and felt standing next to me was almost overwhelming. I understand now how some people can be completely overcome by fear. Of course, the first thing which came out of my mouth was a rebuke in the Name of Jesus. Immediately, the evil spirit was gone.

Over the next month I saw this Spirit of Fear on two more occasions. The second time I saw this Spirit of Fear he walked through the doorway as I laid down on my bed. I immediately rebuked the Spirit as I had done before, and he fled. This time the Spirit only managed to get two or three steps inside the door.

On the third and last occasion I encountered this devil, I had just laid down when I saw him coming from a distance. I recognized it immediately as a Spirit of Fear. Fear did not come through the door this time, but was walking toward the bedroom wall in front of me.

I watched this Spirit as he walked closer and closer to the wall. This time I noticed he was wearing a hat just like the hat I always wore fishing and/or canoeing. I further noticed he also walked with the same gait as I walked. Except for his hideous looking head and face, he dressed and walked just like I did. I watched this Spirit as he came closer and closer. This Spirit of Fear finally reached the wall and started bouncing off the wall. He could not enter into the room because there was a Wall of Faith preventing him from entering the room again.

I knew the Lord was teaching me something through this experience. I rebuked this Spirit of Fear again as I had previously done the other two times, and immediately he disappeared. Since that night, I have never again encountered the Spirit of Fear in this way. The first and second time I encountered the Spirit of Fear, he was able to enter the room through the doorway because I had left a door open for him to come in. If we have fear in our life, it is because we have left a door open for it to come through.

All evil spirits enter through doorways in our minds which we leave open and unattended. If we have faith, the Spirit of Fear has no doorway by which it can enter. If fear tries to enter our mind another way, a Wall of Faith can stop it from doing so. This is called our SHEILD OF FAITH. Many Christians are not utilizing the WHOLE ARMOR OF GOD. If we are fearful we are not rooted and grounded in the Tree of Life. If we are walking with Christ daily we have nothing to fear.

Faith is like a wall or shield of protection. That is why Paul said we have been given THE SHIELD OF FAITH. Demon spirits cannot enter in through a wall or Shield of Faith. Fear can only enter through the doors we leave open and unattended. The only power the enemy possesses in our life is the power we allow him to have.

The enemy comes to steal our peace through various trials, tests and temptations. However, PEACE LIKE A RIVER will flow within the hearts of those who make the Prince of Peace their Habitation. The Love of Christ will cast out all fear as we partake of the Tree of Life daily. Christ is our Peace and we live in Peace because we are communing with Him daily.

A year or so after seeing this devil, my mother, who has since went home to be with Jesus, told me about a similar experience she had with a Spirit of Fear. I had never told her about the Spirit I saw, but the Spirit she saw looked exactly like the one I had seen.

She had seen a Spirit of Fear not long after my Father had gone home to be with the Lord. She was in bed when a Spirit of Fear appeared before her bedside. She said the evil spirit came into the room and stood beside her bed. She described this Spirit as having no eyes, nose, mouth or ears. She said all she could think to do was pray. She said after praying the Spirit went away.

My mother was of the Baptist Faith and had not been taught, or had any knowledge about demon spirits and spiritual warfare. However, she knew what she needed to do. Fear can bring torment if you allow it to, but prayer can bring peace. If fear can find an open door, it will always enter in to bring torment.

Fear can bind and hinder us from receiving instruction and guidance from God. When God gives us a mandate, we must trust that He will provide every need we have to perform that task, no matter where He may send us or what He tells us to do.

At this particular time in my life I was getting ready to move to another state and was unsure if this move was of God. Abraham, not knowing where God was leading him, was moved by faith to receive the land of his inheritance. Sometimes God gives us a word we can stand on with step by step instructions. Sometimes we just have to go, believing God will show us where to go and what to do as we obey Him. God is always faithful when we are obedient.

Many times I have waited on a word from God or a vision to point me in the right direction. At times God gave me an open vision or a word, but the move has always been the right one. I did not base my decision on a word from God or a vision alone, but upon faith in the fact that He had told me what to do and where to go. I did not have to know and see what was ahead, only that God was leading me there one step at a time.

God rarely shows us or gives us the entire picture when He tells us to do something. Most of the time He gives us direction step by step. Each step can be a miracle which leads us to a greater walk of faith with Him.

The Fear of the unknown is the enemy of our souls. Faith in what I know and who I know will guide me through the unknown. God is love, and faith in His Love for us will cast out all fear and intimidation. The Devil would not try to stop us from fulfilling the plan of God if the move we are about to make is not of God. God will always give us His Peace concerning His will for our life. In my confrontation with the Spirit of

Fear God revealed to me how fear affects us and impacts the decisions we make.

FEAR NOT

God repeatedly tells us in His Word to "FEAR NOT." We need to grab hold of all the FEAR NOTS and trust God. Faith, not fear, needs to be written on the BANNER of our hearts so we can defeat the Spirit of Fear when he tries to influence our decisions. When fear comes knocking at the door, we can use the Word of God to defend our territory. Truth transforms us into the image of Christ. Satan cannot get past the Blood of Jesus and the Cross embellished on the doorposts of our hearts.

Fear always challenges and confronts the Word of God which is the Sword of the Spirit as well as our Shield of Faith. Fear always intimidates, antagonizes, and probes the strongholds of our Faith in an effort to find any weaknesses we may have in our defenses. Fear always questions the integrity of God and His Word. FAITH CANNOT FAIL, and will not fail when our Faith is established on the tried and true Foundation of Truth. Christ our Redeemer is the Truth which sets us free from the torment of fear.

The reason the Spirit of Fear has no eyes, nose, mouth or ears is because it does not need any of these features. It utilizes your mouth, eyes, nose, and/or ears. The Scripture tells us "not to be afraid of sudden fear when it comes upon you." Proverbs, Chapter 3, Verse 25. Fear will surely come knocking at the door of your heart. However, if Fear senses the Blood of Jesus on the doorpost of your heart it will flee in terror.

We are either justified or condemned by the words we speak. We will be delivered to our tormentor if out of fear we choose to speak the words of doubt, defeat and unbelief. If the power of the tongue produces life and death, then WE MUST choose the Words of Life and not Death. Words of Life and Faith will always counteract the words of Death and Fear.

The Spirit of Fear ALWAYS uses our own words and actions to condemn and defeat us if we are weak in Faith. What shall we eat, drink or wear? How will we pay our bills? Am I going to die? Will I live long enough to die??????? How will it all end? Where is God who swore to protect us? Why did God allow this to happen to me? Fear always questions the integrity of God's Word and the relevance of His promises to His children.

We speak our own demise when we align our thoughts, words, actions and ideas with our enemy, Satan. REMEMBER, WHOEVER WINS THE BATTLE OF THE MIND IS THE ONE WHO WILL TAKE THE SPOILS AND CONTROL THE LIFE OF AN INDIVIDUAL." Faith is the VICTORY which overcomes the World." Either we have faith--OR--we do not have faith! If we find ourselves lacking in faith, it is obtainable if we will seek Christ who is our "source of Faith." God offers us mountain moving faith enabling us to cast off the works of darkness and perform the miraculous.

The enemy would have us believe that MOUNTAIN MOVING FAITH is not obtainable and something which is beyond our grasp in this life. However, SATAN IS A LIAR. Christ said if we have Faith as a grain of mustard seed, we can speak to the mountain and command it to be cast into the sea, and it WILL BE DONE. God gives us all a measure of faith and tells us to seek greater Faith so we may obtain grace and find help in the time of need. Faith, as a grain of mustard seed, can move a mountain so why do men whine and whimper at the sight of a mole hill?

The Spirit of Fear has no eyes because it has no need of eyes. This Spirit has no need of eyes because it uses the eyes of the victim as its own. The Spirit of Fear when it comes upon its victim will always cause the victim to magnify and focus on the problem rather than the solution. On the other hand, faith will always focus on the solution and magnify the person who is the solution, Christ Jesus.

A fearful individual can only see what fear desires him to see if he allows fear to enter into his heart. In a fearful heart the solution, Faith, is not apparent because fear has confused the mind with unbelief, doubt and despair. Fear uses our eyes to blind us from seeing the ONLY answer to every problem. JESUS IS THE ANSWER. Jesus is the ANSWER to every situation which arises in our life.

Fear beguiles the heart, blinds spiritual eyes, deafens spiritual ears and hinders Truth from proceeding from our mouth. In other words, fear confuses the spiritual senses and shuts down the process of Faith within us. Thus, people have trouble believing in the ANSWER which is Christ Jesus. Out of the abundance of a beguiled heart, the mouth fearfully speaks.

The Spirit of Fear does not have ears because it does not need ears. He uses your ears to hear what he desires you to hear. When the Spirit of Fear comes upon an individual, the individual can only hear what the Spirit of Fear desires him or her to hear. WHAT THE SPIRIT OF FEAR DESIRES THE INDIVIDUAL TO HEAR IS THAT PERSON'S OWN WORDS AS HE SPEAKS DOUBT, DEFEAT, DOOM, DESPAIR GLOOM AND AGONY ON ME!

OUT OF THE ABUNDANCE OF THE HEART THE MOUTH SPEAKS. Matthew, Chapter 12, Verse 34. If our heart is filled with fear, we have been taken captive by the Spirit of Fear. The Spirit of Fear can, and will control the direction we take when we encounter problems, tests and trials if we allow it to.

A FOOL'S MOUTH IS HIS DESTRUCTION AND HIS LIPS ARE THE SNARE OF HIS SOUL. Proverbs, Chapter 18, Verse 2. Our own words can become the very thing which places us in bondage to the Spirit of Fear or sets us free from bondage. When we speak, however, we must not let the words we speak be the words chosen by our enemy. If we allow the enemy to choose our words, we have already joined him in conquering our minds, thus allowing his kingdom to rule and reign over our thoughts and control our life.

No matter what the circumstances may be, we MUST be vigilant in our efforts to destroy any inclination of fear in our life. When the enemy comes in like a flood, we must LIFT UP A STANDARD AGAINST HIM and stand firm in our Faith in the FINISHED WORKS OF CHRIST. PERFECT LOVE CASTS OUT ALL FEAR. (See 1 John ch. 4 vs. 18). When the love of God dwells within us richly, fear cannot have dominion over us.

Our hearts will be established in PERFECT PEACE if we allow the PERFECT PEACE of God to rule and reign in our hearts. We must come to the realization that the DEVIL is more afraid of us than we are of him. When you stand firm in your Faith in Christ, your enemy cannot torment you because you have no fear of him.

CHAPTER 11

THE PATH MOST TRAVELED

THERE IS A WAY (path) THAT SEEMETH RIGHT UNTO MAN, BUT THE END THEREOF ARE THE WAYS OF DEATH. Proverbs, Chapter 14, Verse 12.

There is a Path many men walk which seems to them to be the right path. Unfortunately, the Path they have chosen is leading them toward damnation, death and destruction. The Path Least Traveled is the PATH OF LIFE. The Path of Life leads to the Tree of Life which is Jesus Christ. The Path which most men follow is the Path which leads to the Tree of the Knowledge of Good and Evil.

THE PATH MOST TRAVELED is the Path which is rooted and grounded in the Tree of the Knowledge of Good and Evil. Everything found along this Path is designed to lead one AWAY from the Tree of Life. This Path is a BROAD Path with many demonic and treacherous twists and turns. It is the Path chosen by the Masses.

WHEREFORE SEEING WE ALSO ARE COMPASSED ABOUT WITH SO GREAT A CLOUD OF WITNESSES LET US LAY ASIDE EVERY WIEIGHT, AND THE SIN WHICH DOES SO EASILY BESET US AND LET US RUN WITH PATIENCE THE RACE THAT IS SET BEFORE US. Hebrews, Chapter 12, Verse 1.

Everyone is running a spiritual race. In life there are paths that lead in many different directions. However, there are only two Paths which lead men to their spiritual destiny. There is a right Path which men can choose to follow in order to receive a Crown of Life. There is a wrong Path many men choose to follow which leads to destruction, death and the Lake of Fire. To win the race and a Crown of Life men must run with patient endurance until they reach the Finnish Line.

THE DREAM

During the Christmas Season I had a dream in which I was walking through a large Shopping Center. People were scurrying through the Mall going from shop to shop for something to purchase. Their minds were not on the true meaning of Christmas, but on the gifts they could find for themselves and for others.

After passing several stores in the Mall, I finally came to the end of the Shopping Center. I walked through a doorway at the end of the Mall into a very large room. The ceiling in the room seemed to be at least thirty feet high.

There was a large brick wall in front of me which started turning different colors. They were all very brilliant colors. The wall changed from one color to another. Finally the wall turned from a beautiful deep purple to a brilliant gold color. Above me, a large television screen appeared in the middle of the wall.

I was so excited because I just knew God had a message for me!!! Indeed, He did have a message for me; however, it was not the type of message I was hoping it would be. I thought God was about to give me some great revelation about my ministry, and hopefully, new direction for my life. However, the message I received from Him was not for me or about me. The message He gave me was about the condition of His Church and of the Leaders of His Church.

Images of different Preachers began appearing before me on the large screen. At first the Preachers were saying things that sounded reasonable. Each Preacher had something to say which seemed relevant for today. As the screen went from Preacher to Preacher and frame to frame, the words they were saying became distorted.

What seemed at first to be a message from God had turned into something sinister and deceiving. The words they were speaking grieved my spirit, and I became irritated and angry at what these Preachers were saying. I felt like if I stayed there any longer I was going to explode.

Suddenly, a hideous looking character appeared on the screen above me and began speaking to me about death. I could not stand to listen to him any longer because his words were vexing my spirit. I knew I was dreaming and I began shaking myself out of a deep sleep. I knew the Lord was trying to reveal something important to me. I immediately began asking the Lord for the interpretation of the dream. I got out of bed and began to write the dream in my notebook.

The dream was about the Tree of the Knowledge of Good and Evil and its deceptive powers. In the Garden of Eden the Serpent beguiled Eve into thinking there was no harm in disobeying the Commandment of God. The Serpent told Eve that the Forbidden Fruit on the Tree would make her wise. Eve looked at the Tree and saw "THAT IT WAS PLEASANT TO THE EYES AND A TREE TO THAT WAS GOOD FOR FOO." (See Genesis ch. 3 vs. 6).

There are many trees and plants in the World which bear pleasant looking fruit. However, some fruit looks good to the eye, but is bitter to the taste. Just because fruit may be pleasant to look at does not mean it is "good for food." Many people have died from eating plants and berries which look good, but contain bitterness and even deadly poisons.

Everything the Preachers were saying on the television screen seemed believable, just like the Serpent's beguiling

Sermon to Eve regarding the Forbidden Fruit. IN THE BEGINNING their words sounded very promising but contained only a hint of truth. Even the walls around the television screen in the large room were encased in beautiful brilliant colors. Some of the colors were the colors which represent the Divine Nature of Christ and His position of Royalty in Heavenly Places. However everything was just a facade.

All the beauty which surrounded the words coming from the television screen was just a veil hiding the BITTER FRUIT which the tongue of Satan's earthly Serpents were spewing out of their mouths. Gold represents the Divine Nature of Christ Jesus. Fool's Gold is found in the mouths of fools. What lies behind the veil of deception is what leads men to the pit of death and destruction. A FOOL'S MOUTH IS HIS DESTRUCTION, AND HIS LIPS ARE THE SNARE OF HIS SOUL. Proverbs, Chapter 18, Verse 7.

Not all that looks good is good. Not all that glitters is gold. The STREETS OF GOLD in Heaven are made of "clear gold." Gold, in its purest form, is transparent. The Serpent's gold may glitter, but it is a counterfeit which obscures the truth. Not all that feels good is good. Not all that sounds good is good. What is behind the VEIL OF DECEPTION always leads to death and destruction.

THE WIDE GATE

ENTER YE IN AT THE STRAIGHT GATE: FOR WIDE IS THE GATE, THAT LEADETH TO DESTRUCTION, AND MANY THERE BE WHICH GO IN THEREAT. BECAUSE STRAIGHT IS THE GATE, AND NARROW IS THE WAY, WHICH LEADETH UNTO LIFE, AND FEW THERE BE THAT FIND IT. BEWARE OF FALSE PROPHETS, WHICH COME TO YOU IN SHEEP'S CLOTHING, BUT INWARDLY THEY ARE RAVENING WOLVES. Matthew, Chapter 7, Verses 13-15.

All false religions and doctrines are veiled with what looks like, sounds like and feels like the Truth. The Tree of Life is the only place where Truth can be found. The Foundation of all Truth is rooted and grounded in the Tree of Life.

All false doctrines and religions are rooted and grounded in the Tree of the Knowledge of Good and Evil. If we allow the Serpent to take our focus off the Tree of Life, we will find ourselves on the PATH MOST TRAVELED, which is the Broad Path leading to death and destruction.

The Wide Path veils many pitfalls and is littered with the filthiness of flesh and debaucheries of this present World. There is no escaping the judgment of sin which lies down the road for all who persist in traveling the PATH MOST TRAVELED. Along this Path many snares are buried under the guise of earthly pleasures and treasures designed to lead men to a hellish destination.

There are many trees along the PATH MOST TRAVELED which bear poisonous fruit. The fruit on these trees may look GOOD FOR FOOD, but eating their fruit will surely bring death to all who eat of them.

The fruit we have chosen to eat along our way will determine where our journey ends. The fruit we are eating either comes from the Tree of Life or the Tree of the Knowledge of Good and Evil.

THE PATH MOST TRAVELED is a deceptive one. Along this Path things are not always the way they seem. There are many satanically inspired traps along this Path which lead to death and destruction. Deception is the name of the Serpent's game which leads mankind to sorrow and shame. However, there is hope for all who will repent and change the course of their earthly travels.

CHAPTER 12

THE PATH LEAST TRAVELED

ENTER YE IN AT THE STRAIGHT GATE: FOR WIDE IS THE GATE, AND BROAD IS THE WAY, THAT LEADETH TO DE-STRUCTION, AND MANY THEREBE WHICH GO IN THEREAT: BECAUSE STRAIGHT IS THE GATE: AND NARROW IS THE WAY, WHICH LEADETH UNTO LIFE, AND FEW THERE BE THAT FIND IT. Matthew, Chapter 7, Verses 13-14.

The PATH LEAST TRAVELED is the Path to the Tree of Life. The Cross is the Path leading to the Tree which bears the Fruit of Eternal Life. Jesus is the only one qualified to lead us down this Path. He is the TRUTH, THE LIFE and THE WAY. He is the RESUR-RECTION and the LIFE. Jesus takes us down the NARROW PATH which leads to the STRAIGHT GATE and Eternal Life. The Narrow Path holds the keys which leads to all Heavenly Blessings.

Jesus said: "I AM THE DOOR OF THE SHEEP." The actual Greek reads: "I am the GATE of the sheep." Although the PATH LEAST TRAVELED is narrow, it is the only Path which leads to the GATE, "JESUS." Few people are interested in finding this narrow path because they are too busy with all the deceptive distrac-tions and pleasures they encounter on the BROAD WAY which leads to death.

THE LORD IS MY SHEPHERD; I SHALL NOT WANT (lack). HE MAKETH ME TO LIE DOWN IN GREEN PASTURES: HE LEADETH ME BESIDE THE STILL WATERS. HE RESTORETH MY SOUL: HE LEADETH ME IN PATHS OF RIGHTEOUSNESS FOR HIS NAME'S SAKE. Psalms, 23, Verses 1-3.

The PATH LEAST TRAVELED is a righteous one. It is a HOLY HIGHWAY which leads to Eternal Life in Christ Jesus. Not many are willing to pay the price to walk in Holiness. Along the Highway of Holiness we learn to be obedient and faithful to His call. If we hunger and thirst after righteousness, we will be filled with all the Heavenly Treasures of the DIVINE NATURE OF CHRIST.

Man's greatest Treasure is God's plan and purpose for his life. Man's greatest purpose is to walk a path in communion and fellowship with God. This is why our obedience to Him is of the utmost importance. The Law of Sin and Death, which is a consequence for eating the Forbidden Fruit, alienates us from fulfilling the call of God on our life. When we deny Christ access to our life, we travel the Path which leads to destruction.

Abraham sojourned in the land God promised him, but was continuously looking for that Heavenly City God was preparing for His people. He was looking for a Heavenly inheritance as his final resting place. He wasn't satisfied with things which were temporal. He never ceased searching for that City while he was on Earth.

Abraham's eyes were focused on the path which led to righteousness rather than the one which led to self-righteousness and destruction. He rejoiced to see "THE DAY OF CHRIST, SAW IT AND WAS GLAD." John, Chapter 8, Verse 56. By Faith Abraham received the promise of a Savior who had not yet been born or died on the Cross.

The PATH LEAST TRAVELED is the Path which leads to Living Water. Along the Path is a River of Life-giving Water which never runs dry. Living Water produces the understanding we need as we drink from this FOUNTAIN OF LIFE.

SELF–DENIAL

IN HIM WAS LIFE AND; AND THE LIFE WAS THE LIGHT (understanding) OF MEN. John, Chapter 1, Verse 4. When we are exposed to True Light, the Path on which we are walking becomes illuminated. Christ is the Light which enlightens the "eyes of our understanding" along the WAY. That Path leads us to NEWNESS OF LIFE AND SPIRIT WE FIND IN CHRIST JESUS. Romans, Chapter 6, Verse 4; Chapter 7, Verse 6.

THE PATH LEAST TRAVELED is the path of self-denial. Jesus said: IF ANY MAN WILL COME AFTER ME, LET HIM DENY HIMSELF, AND TAKE UP HIS CROSS AND FOLLOW ME. FOR WHOSOEVER WILL SAVE HIS LIFE SHALL LOSE IT; AND WHOSOEVER WILL LOSE HIS LIFE FOR MY SAKE WILL FIND IT. Matthew, Chapter 16, Verses 24-25. Like Christ, we have been called to a life of sacrifice and self-denial.

Self-denial is the Path few will Travel. In denying ourselves, we become Christ-centered rather than self-centered. Self-centeredness always looks inwardly to the needs and desires of one's self. Christ-centeredness always focuses on the Tree of Life and the needs of others.

To walk the PATH LEAST TRAVELED we must die to our own Will and desires so that the Life and Light of Christ can lead us down the Path of TRUTH, RIGHTEOUSNESS AND FAITH. To "lose your life" means to relinquish control of your life to Christ so the plan and purpose of God can be fulfilled within you. Many are called to walk the PATH LEAST TRAVELED, however, few are chosen. Many are rejected because many choose to follow the desires of their own hearts.

THOU WILT SHOW ME THE PATH OF LIFE: IN THY PRESENCE IS FULLNESS OF JOY; AT THY RIGHT HAND THERE ARE PLEASURES EVERMORE. Psalms, 16, Verse 11.

The PATH LEAST TRAVELED is also the Path where we find the JOY OF THE LORD. It is the JOY of the Lord which is our strength. God desires that we be filled with His Joy—a Joy which is unspeakable and full of HIS GLORY. He gave us the Commandment to LOVE ONE ANOTHER in order that our joy can be full.

There is a JOY which cannot be described when we are eating from the Tree of Life. If you could bottle this Joy, it would be priceless. However, this Joy cannot be bottled and sold. Jesus already paid for our Joy at Calvary. This Joy is free to all who walk the PATH LEAST TRAVELED.

On the PATH LEAST TRAVELED we find Wisdom. FOR THE LORD GIVETH WISDOM: OUT OF HIS MOUTH COMETH KNOWL-EDGE AND UNDERSTANDING. HE LAYETH UP SOUND WISDOM FOR THE RIGHTEOUS: HE IS A BUCKLER TO THEM THAT WALK UPRIGHTLY. HE KEEPETH THE PATHS OF JUDGMENT, AND PER-SERVETH THE WAY OF HIS SAINTS. THEN SHALL THOU UNDER-STAND RIGHTEOUSNESS AND JUDGMENT, AND EQUITY; YEA, EVERY GOOD PATH. Proverbs, Chapter 2, Verses 6-9.

The PATH LEAST TRAVELED IS THE HIGHWAY OF HOLI-NESS. Without Holiness no man can walk with God in His Heavenly Paradise. Without Holiness no man can see God or know Him as He truly is. The Path to true Wisdom leads us to the Cross of Christ.

Not many would walk the Path of Wisdom. The Wisdom of this World is rooted and grounded in the Tree of the Knowledge of Good and Evil. Eve saw that the Fruit was GOOD FOR FOOD AND ONE THAT WOULD MAKE HER WISE. However, it was an earthly wisdom. The wisdom of this world is sensual and devilish. (see James Ch. 3, Vs. 15). The wisdom of this world is filled with deadly poisons which lead to the death, destruction and eternal punishment of men.

We obtain Faith, Knowledge and Understanding through Wisdom. Jesus Christ is our Wisdom. If we are following Him down the PATH LEAST TRAVELED, we will find Life Eternal and Joy Unspeakable which is FULL OF HIS GLORY.

Those who walk the PATH LEAST TRAVELED do not follow the Masses. They focus on the Tree of Life, Christ. Those who are led by the Spirit will walk in the Spirit. As long as they keep their eyes on the Tree of Life which is before them, they will not be influenced or beguiled by worldly pleasures and deceptive treasures.

THE PATH OF LOVE

Finally, THE PATH LEAST TRAVELED is the Path of Love. BELOVED, LET US LOVE ONE ANOTHER: FOR LOVE IS OF GOD; AND EVERYONE THAT LOVETH IS BORN OF GOD, AND KNOWETH GOD. HE THAT LOVETH NOT KNOWETH NOT GOD; FOR GOD IS LOVE. 1 John, Chapter 3, Verses 7-8.

Without Love the Message of the Cross becomes void and of no affect. The Message of the Cross is the witness and the confirmation of the Love God has for His Beloved. The Path of Love will always lead to Christ and what He did at Calvary. For Christ, the Path to the Cross was a Path of Suffering and Shame. The Cross is the Path to Salvation for all who believe in Him.

The Path of Love leads us to the Throne Room of God where we can come boldly before Him in the time of need. For us, it is a Path of self-denial and humility. Loving God, loving the Brethren and loving others is the highest calling we can obtain.

As we walk the PATH OF GOD'S LOVE, His Love constrains and compels us to "love one another." We are made complete in His love when we determine that we are going to walk down this Path with Him. God has promised to give us the desires of our heart when we seek Him with all diligence. Christ becomes the desire of our heart when we realize the greatest gift we can obtain is the gift of HIS LOVE.

When we walk the PATH LEAST TRAVELED, we become Samaritans along the Jericho Road. We will help others along the way who have been victimized by the evil intentions and attacks of the enemy. As we go into all the World and share the Gospel of the Kingdom of God with those who do not know Him, we are fulfilling the GREAT COMMISION.

LOVE seeks not its own, but the welfare and wellbeing of others. LOVE seeks no reward of its own, but seeks to establish God's Love and Righteousness in others. True Love is more than just an emotion. True Love is something that becomes a daily lifestyle as we walk the PATH LEAST TRAVELED.

The Bible states that "GOD IS LOVE." 1 John Chapter 4, Verse 8. Unlike man, God's Love is unconditional. It does not seek the approval or affections of anyone else. God's Love is not a sensuous type of love which the world embraces, but a self-denial type of love. His Love is rooted in Grace and Mercy.

GRACE and MERCY sit on the THRONE OF LOVE. God has placed His Love in our hearts. LIVING WATERS will flow from a heart full of LOVE if we are rooted and grounded in Christ. His LOVE always looks for an opportunity to display GRACE and MERCY. LOVE IS OPTIMISTIC. LOVE IS KIND. LOVE REJOICES IN TRUTH. LOVE NEVER FAILS. 1 Corinthians, Chapter 13, Verses 4-8.

CHAPTER 13

THE SEED AND THE CROSS

AND THE LORD SAID UNTO THE SERPENT, BECAUSE THOU HAST DONE THIS, THOU ART CURSED ABOVE EVERY BEAST OF THE FIELD; UPON THY BELLY SHALT THOU GO, AND DUST SHALT THOU EAT ALL THE DAYS OF THY LIFE: AND I WILL PUT ENMITY BETWEEN THEE AND THE WOMAN, AND BETWEEN THY SEED AND HER SEED; IT SHALL BRUISE THY HEAD AND THOU SHALT BRUISE HIS HEEL. Genesis, Chapter 3, Verses 1415.

The Seed of the Woman is Christ Jesus, the second Adam. The Second Adam, Christ, had the power to prevail over the Serpent's temptation. The first Adam failed because he succumbed to the Serpent's temptation and ate of the Tree of the Knowledge of Good and Evil. Christ was the Seed which was sown in the Earth in order to bruise the head of the Serpent. What the Serpent did to mankind in the Garden of Eden, Christ did to the Serpent at Calvary.

Bruising the head of the Serpent at Calvary turned the tables of confusion on the Kingdom of Darkness. Had the Princes of Darkness known what they were doing at Calvary, they would have never crucified Christ. No weapon that is formed against us can prosper because the Seed of Christ which dwells within us KEEPS and sustains us. The schemes of the enemy cannot prevail against us when we have made Christ Jesus our Fortress, Buckler and Shield.

One night the Lord spoke to me in a dream saying: EX-CEPT A GRAIN OF WHEAT FALLS TO THE GROUND AND DIES IT CANNOT BRING FORTH FRUIT. (See John ch. 12 vs. 24). As I slept the words of this scripture was repeating over and over in my mind. When I woke up in the morning, these words continued resounding in my spirit.

THE HOUR IS COME, THAT THE SON OF MAN SHOULD BE GLORIFIED. John, Chapter 12, Verse 23. Jesus was speaking concerning His death, burial and resurrection. He likened His death and resurrection to being glorified. Continuing, He said: VERILY, VERILY I SAY UNTO YOU, EXCEPT A GRAIN (SEED) OF WHEAT FALL TO THE GROUND AND DIE, IT ABIDETH ALONE: BUT IF IT DIES, IT BRINGETH FORTH MUCH FRUIT. John, Chapter 12, Verse 24.

Christ, the Seed of Life, was put to death on the Cross, planted into the ground and was raised from the dead on the third day. Jesus was raised from the dead in order to produce a great HARVEST OF SOULS.

Seeds produce after their own kind. If I plant wheat seeds in the ground, I can expect a harvest of wheat. The same is true with corn or any other kind of seeds. WHATEVER WE SOW--WE WILL REAP. Galatians Chapter 6, Verse 7.

The Miracle of the Seed is that it has to die first and then be planted into the ground, before it can produce a bountiful harvest. The Seed of Life, Christ, had to die before Life could be reproduced in mankind. The Seed of Life, Christ, was the Seed of Hope for all who would believe on the name of the Lord Jesus Christ. That Seed had to be nailed to the Cross to bear the sins of all mankind so that all who would believe in Him could find Eternal Life.

Each of our lives are like seeds which have been sown in earthly places. Before we can find Everlasting Life in Christ, we must die to this present World. We must pick up our Cross daily and follow in His footsteps. If we are to be fruitful in Christ, we must deny ourselves and put to death the Works of the Flesh.

> NOW THE WORKS OF THE FLESH ARE MANIFEST, WHICH ARE THESE: FORNICATION, UNCLEANNESS, LACIVIOUSNESS, ADULTRY, IDOLATRY, WITCHCRAFT, HATRED, VARIANCE, EMULATIONS, WRATH, STRIFE, SEDITIONS, HERISIES, ENVEYINGS, REVELINGS, AND SUCH LIKE: OF THE WHICH I TELL YOU BEFORE, AS I HAVE ALSO TOLD YOU IN TIMES PAST, THAT THEY WHICH DO THESE THINGS SHALL NOT ENTER INTO THE KINGDOM OF GOD. Galatians, Chapter 5, Verses 19-21.

THE STORY OF THE CROSS

The last book I wrote was entitled "THE STORY OF THE CROSS." It is a Story about an Olive Tree which grew up on the Mount of Olives just outside of Jerusalem. In the book this Olive Tree eventually became the Cross on which Jesus was crucified. It was written from the viewpoint of the Cross and what he would have seen, felt and experienced if he had been a person.

In reality, as Christians, we WERE that Cross on which Christ died. We (our sins) were the burden Jesus carried to the Cross on Mount Calvary. We were the reason He suffered, bled and died. The Apostle Paul said: "I AM CRUCIFIED WITH CHRIST: NEVERTHELESS I LIVE; YET NOT I, BUT CHRIST LIVETH IN ME." Galatians, Chapter 2, Verse 20. On the Cross Christ became the "curse of sin" for the sins of ALL mankind.

In the Bible trees and wood, in general, are prophetic of mankind. For many years the Scriptures have been written on paper which is byproduct of wood. This also is symbolic of God's Word being written on and established in our hearts when we become believers in Jesus Christ.

The ARK OF THE COVEANANT was made out of wood and overlaid with gold. Gold represents the DIVINE NATURE OF CHRIST. The wooden Ark was a type and shadow of mankind's heart which would one day be a vessel containing the Word of God. The Ten Commandments, the Showbread and Aaron's Rod which budded were placed in the Ark. The presence of God dwelt in the Ark as a type and shadow of things to come.

In the Bible there are several references where the Cross is referred to as a "tree." We cannot deny that it was man's sins that nailed Christ to the Cross.

When we see the Revelation of Christ upon the Cross as our Redeemer, we know that we are the focus of His love. Our sins became the instrument of His death. Christ who knew no sin became sin so that we could be called the "RIGHTEOUSNESS OF GOD IN HIM." HE WAS WOUNDED FOR OUR TRANSGRESSIONS AND BRUISED FOR OUR INIQUITES.

When we experience the Revelation of the Cross and accept Jesus Christ as our Lord and Savior, like Paul, we can also say "I HAVE BEEN CRUCIFIED WITH CHRIST." If we had no sin, there would have been no need for Christ to be crucified.

In the Garden of Eden Christ was represented as the Tree of Life. The Tree of the Knowledge of Good and Evil represented Satan and the Law of Sin and Death. Unfortunately, we came under the judgment of the Forbidden Tree and what that tree represented because of sin.

The Cross was also a representation of the Law of Sin and Death. The consequence of sin is always Death. Someone had to pay the penalty for sin. Like Adam and Eve, the fig leaves I tried to hide my sin with did not hide or wash away my guilt and shame.

At Calvary we see the Tree of Life and the Tree of the Knowledge of Good and Evil meeting together in conflict. It was the Law of Life verses the Law of Sin and Death. For a brief period of time it looked as though Life had lost and Death had won. However, behind the scenes the SEED OF LIFE was fulfilling its mandate to produce a Harvest of Life Everlasting.

The Tree of Life had to be nailed to the Tree which represented the Law of Sin and Death. FOR HE HAS MADE HIM TO BE SIN FOR US WHO KNEW NO SIN THAT WE MIGHT BE MADE THE RIGHTEOUSNESS OF GOD IN HIM. 2 Corinthians, Chapter 5, Verse 21. This was the Plan of God from the beginning. When God told the Serpent the woman's seed, Christ, would bruise his head, He was revealing His Plan of Redemption for mankind. (Gen. ch. 3, vs. 15) He who knew no sin became sin. Christ became the curse of sin in order that sin would no longer have dominion over us.

CHRIST HATH REDEEMED US FROM THE LAW, BEING MADE A CURSE FOR US: FOR IT IS WRITTEN, CURSED EVERY-ONE THAT HANGETH ON A TREE. Galatians, Chapter 3, Verse 13. Christ was the promised Seed that hung upon the Tree (Cross) so the promise of justification by faith could be realized. NOW TO ABRAHAM AND HIS SEED WERE THE PROMISES MADE. HE SAID NOT, AND TO THE SEEDS, AS OF MANY; BUT AS ONE, AND TO THY SEED, WHICH IS CHRIST. Galatians, Chapter 3, Verse 16.

It was an imperfect man that sinned. It took a perfect man who knew no sin, Christ, to become sin and reverse the curse OF sin for all who would believe in Him. In His flesh He became the mediator between man and God. WHO HIS OWN SELF BARE OUR SINS IN HIS OWN BODY ON THE TREE, THAT WE, BEING DEAD TO SIN, SHOULD LIVE UNTO RIGHTEOUSNESS: BY WHOSE STRIPES YE WERE HEALED. 1 Peter, Chapter 2, Verse 24.

The conflagration between man and God is now a conflict between man with God (believers) against the Serpent and his seed. The seed of the Serpent is the Seed of Confusion and Beguilement which tempted Eve to EAT OF THE FORBIDDEN FRUIT in the beginning.

The seed of the Serpent is the Spirit of Anti-Christ. This seed will eventually find its ultimate residence in "THE SON OF PERDITION." However, the SEED (Christ) AND THE CROSS will eventually prevail over the Kingdom of Darkness and the seed of the Serpent at the END OF DAYS. Our victory has already been confirmed at the Cross. "THERE IS NO WEAPON THAT IS FORMED AGAINST US THAT CAN PROSPER AND EVERY TONGUE THAT RISES UP TO JUDGE US WILL BE CONDEMNED BY US." (See Isaiah ch. 54 vs. 17).

Faith in the Power of the Cross and the Seed of Life, Christ, who dwells within us, is our assurance and hope of Glory. Jesus prayed: THAT THEY ALL MAY BE ONE: AS THOU, FATHER, ART IN ME, AND I IN THEE, THAT THEY ALSO MAY BE ONE IN US: THAT THE WORLD MAY BELIEVE THAT THOU HAST SENT ME. AND THE GLORY WHICH THOU HAST GAVEST ME I HAVE GIVEN THEM; THAT THEY MAY BE ONE, EVEN AS WE ARE ONE. John, Chapter 17, Verses 21-22. HE THAT HATH AN EAR, LET HIM HEAR WHAT THE SPIRIT SAITH UNTO THE CHURCHES; TO HIM THAT OVERCOMETH WILL I GIVE TO EAT OF THE TREE OF LIFE, WHICH IS IN THE MIDST OF THE PARADISE OF GOD. Revelation, Chapter 2, Verse 7.

The TREE OF LIFE was found in the Garden of Eden. Eden means "delight and pleasure." Eden was Adam's Garden of Delight and Pleasure. More than anything, we need to remember that Eden was a SPIRITUAL PLACE where the Presence of God dwelt and communed with Adam.

Jesus said in Revelation, Chapter 2, Verse 7, that the Tree of Life was in Paradise. According to Strong's Concordance, another word for Paradise is Eden. In communing and fellowshipping with God, we are eating from the Tree of Life. There is no stronger link between man and God than worship and communion with Him.

The Blood of Jesus is that bond which empowers us to not only believe in God, but to also have fellowship with Him.

We fellowship with Him because the Spirit of Wisdom and Revelation has removed the veil which separated us from knowing Christ and the Power of His Resurrection.

The Apostle Paul prayed: THE GOD OF OUR LORD JESUS CHRIST, THE FATHER OF GLORY, MAY GIVE UNTO YOU THE SPIRIT OF WISDOM AND REVELATION IN THE KNOWLEDGE OF HIM. Ephesians, Chapter 1, Verse 17. All revelation of Christ, who He is and what He has done for us, comes by way of the Spirit of Wisdom and Revelation. Revelation means "an unveiling."

Revelation is something that cannot be taught. It is revealed to us by the Spirit of Truth. Christ is our Wisdom. If we are lacking Wisdom, all we have to do is ask for it without wavering. We receive Wisdom as we eat the Fruit of the Tree of Life.

Worship is the highest form of Praise and Adoration. Praise and Adoration is something that cannot be taught. We respond to the move of God in our hearts as we acknowledge His Presence. We are eating of the Tree of Life when we worship and praise Him in Spirit and in Truth. Praise is not a formula designed to manipulate or please God. It is the heart felt FRUIT of our lips responding to Christ, the "Tree of Life," as we commune with Him intimately.

Access to the Tree of Life has been restored to the descendants of Adam WHO CALL UPON GOD'S NAME. Communion with God is tantamount to eating of the Tree of Life. Through the Power of the Blood of Christ, all who desire may come and "EAT OF THE TREE OF LIFE FREELY."

God's Word is like a beautiful painting. It is like a work of priceless art embellished with life-containing and life sustaining principles that lead us to the Tree of Life. When eating from the Tree of Life, line upon line and precept upon precept, we are engaging ourselves with our Creator in the Splendor of the Paradise of God!

CHAPTER 14

THE SPIRIT OF REVELATION

THAT THE GOD OF OUR LORD JESUS CHRIST, THE FATHER OF GLORY, MAY GIVE UNTO YOU THE SPIRIT OF WISDOM AND REVELATION IN THE KNOWLEDGE OF HIM. Ephesians, Chapter 1, Verse 17.

All spiritual Knowledge, Truth, Understanding and Wisdom are imparted to us by the SPIRIT OF REVELATION. I have been ministering in Churches when God has spoken to me and told me a Spirit of Revelation was present. The Lord desires to impart the fullness of Christ to us through the Spirit of Revelation. He does this by revealing Christ to us in Spirit and Truth.

We gain godly Wisdom through Knowledge and Understanding. Christ, who is our Wisdom, is revealed to us by and through the Spirit of Revelation. We trust Christ because the Spirit of Revelation reveals to us that He is trustworthy. When Jesus asked Peter, "Whom do men say that I am?" Peter replied, "You are the Christ the Son of the Living God." Jesus then said to Peter, "Flesh and blood has not REVEALED THIS TO YOU, but my Father which is in Heaven." (See Matthew ch. 16 vs. 13-20).

Peter's REVELATION of Christ was given by the Spirit of Revelation. The REVELATION of Christ to Peter was not by any means an interpretation of who men believe Christ was or how men may or may not perceive Him. It is the Revelation of the Person of Christ.

The word "revelation" comes from the Greek word "apocalypse" which means an uncovering or unveiling. REVELATION always points us to Truth and Wisdom through Knowledge and Understanding. It is Truth which sets us free, but it is the Spirit of Revelation which reveals to us the Knowledge of the Truth.

The Holy Spirit is the source, bearer and administrator of the Spirit of Revelation. He reveals Christ to us as the personification of all spiritual Truth, Wisdom, Knowledge and Understanding. Without Revelation, we cannot receive Christ as Lord and Savior. The Holy Spirit reveals Christ to us in all His Grace, Majesty and Glory.

Knowledge alone does not give us understanding. Many people have knowledge, however, they do not understand how to apply it properly or to their benefit. Knowledge alone can make one prideful. Understanding and Wisdom will give us the ability to use Knowledge in the proper way. Without Knowledge and Understanding we will surely make decisions which will cause us to fail throughout life.

Many people possess knowledge about Truth (Christ), but they lack Wisdom. They may believe Christ is the Son of God, but they reject Him as Lord and Savior. Satan has knowledge of the Truth, but he cannot accept the Truth. Pride rejects Wisdom, and Wisdom rejects pride. Pride and Wisdom are not compatible with each other. God rejects the proud, but He gives Grace to the humble.

The SPIRIT OF REVELATION directs us to all Truth in order to open the eyes of our understanding enabling us to clearly see and KNOW Christ in all His Glory and Grace. If we are going to experience Christ in the fullness of His Glory and Grace, the Spirit of Revelation must reveal Him to us. The Spirit of Revelation also reveals strategies we can use against the schemes and fiery darts of the Devil.

The Word of Wisdom, Word of Knowledge, and the Discerning of Spirits are Spiritual Gifts imparted to the body of

Christ by the Spirit of Revelation. Whenever the Spirit of Revelation is present, He is there to impart direction, knowledge, wisdom, truth and/or understanding. He comes to reveal the past, present or future to an individual or group of individuals to give hope, direction and/or truth concerning the will, way and purpose of God.

BUT I CERTIFY YOU, BRETHREN, THAT THE GOSPEL WHICH WAS PREACHED OF ME WAS NOT AFTER MAN FOR I NEVER RECEIVED IT OF MAN, NEITHER WAS I TAUGHT IT, BUT BY THE REVELATION OF JESUS CHRIST. Galatians, Chapter 1, Verses 11-12. Revelation is something which cannot be taught. We can tell people about Christ and God's Word. We can teach people what God's Word means and how to walk in victory. However, only the Spirit of Revelation can quicken and cause the Living Word to become alive and a reality in our life.

THE REVELATION OF CHRIST

The MYSTERY of Christ is hidden behind a Veil of Confusion on the Earth. Truth is also like a precious TREASURE hidden in the Earth. If men earnestly desire to KNOW THE TRUTH--they WILL FIND it. Christ is revealed as the Truth, the Life and the REALITY by the Spirit of Revelation. The Holy Spirit is the only one who can reveal Jesus as "CHRIST—THE SON OF THE LIVING GOD."

Understanding that Jesus is the only DOOR to Heaven comes by and through the Spirit of Revelation. When men are drawn to Christ by the Holy Spirit, a door in Heaven is opened in order that they can perceive Christ as REALITY. They then realize Jesus is the only answer for their sin problem.

Many people have knowledge of who Christ is, however, they DO NOT KNOW Him as Lord of Lords and King of Kings. They do not have a Revelation of His true status as Savior and Lord. Their understanding of "who Christ is" and what He did on earth is misunderstood. They know He was a good man who did many good things. However, they do not recognize Him as Lord because they are not eating from the Tree of Life.

Many Christians do not have a full Revelation of Christ and His accomplishments at the Cross. They may know Christ as Lord, but their understanding of many spiritual matters is diminished because they do not pursue a closer relationship with Him. When Christians do not pursue a closer relationship with Him they will not experience Christ in all His fullness.

Many Christians are satisfied with living in the Outer Court of the Temple while others desire to dwell consistently with Christ in the Holiest Place. These Christians are satisfied with living on the outskirts of God's Glory, rarely entering into the Holy of Holies in order to commune with their Creator. Living in the Outer Court can be compared to people living on the outskirts of a beautiful city. These people rarely travel to the HEART of the city where they can experience its beauty and splendor.

Eden was the center of God's will for Adam and Eve. It was the place where the relationship between Adam, Eve and God flourished. Eden was the place where the Shekinah Glory of God dwelt in its fullness. God created The Garden of Eden in order to have a place where He could fellowship with Adam and Eve. His Spirit dwelt with them until their fellowship was abruptly interrupted by the Serpent.

The Presence of God was the center of activity between God and mankind. A Holy Mist, the Shekinah Glory, came out of the ground (heart/spirit) to replenish and renew a daily fellowship with Adam and Eve. The Living Water supplied by the Tree of Life sustained them, causing their relationship with God to bloom and flourish.

KNOW YE NOT THAT YE ARE THE TEMPLE OF GOD,ANDTHAT THE SPIRIT OF GOD DWELLETH IN YOU. 1 Corinthians, Chapter 3, Verse 16. (1 Corinthians, 3:16 is possible because of John, 3:16.) The word "temple" referred to in this scripture comes from the Greek word "Naos" which means Holy of Holies. If we are not living in the Holy of Holies, we are not experiencing the fullness of the Shekinah Glory of God. If we are living in the Outer Court, we are depriving ourselves of the beauty and splendor of an intimate relationship with Christ.

The Spirit of Revelation reveals Christ to us through HIS FINISHED WORKS. Because Christ paid the penalty for our sins, we have access through His Blood to enter into the Holy of Holies. The Holy of Holies represented the Paradise of God where the Presence of God dwelt. God created man so He could dwell with and have fellowship with Him in Paradise. Because of the FINISHED WORKS of CHRIST, man can again dwell in the Paradise of God.

CHAPTER 15

THE FINISHED WORKS

THE SON OF GOD WAS MANIFESTED THAT HE MIGHT DESTROY THE WORKS OF THE DEVIL. 1 John, Chapter 3, Verse 8.

Jesus came to crush the head of the Serpent and RE-VERSE THE CURSE. Christ bore our sins on the Cross and was raised from the dead so mankind could again find the Paradise of God through intimate fellowship and relationship with Him.

FOR GOD SO LOVED THE WORLD, THAT HE GAVE HIS ONLY BEGOTTEN SON, THAT WHOSOEVER BELIEVETH IN HIM SHOULD NOT PERISH, BUT HAVE EVERLASTING LIFE. John, Chapter 3, Verse 16. The concept of Everlasting Life is not only about living forever, but rather about having an everlasting relationship with Jesus Christ. Jesus is our Life. Eternal Life does not exist without Christ. We are the carriers of His Life through the Light of Understanding in the Knowledge of Christ Jesus.

IN CHRIST WAS LIFE AND THAT LIFE WAS THE LIGHT OF MEN. Heaven is the Paradise of God. The Tree of Life does not exist outside the Paradise of God. Jesus has lifted us up to dwell with Him in Heavenly Places far above all principalities and powers. We dwell with Him in Heavenly Places because His Life and Light brings us Eternal Life and Understanding. The Tree of Life dwells in the heart of all who accept Christ as their Lord and Savior.

BLESSED ARE THEY THAT DO HIS COMMANDMENTS, THAT THEY MAY HAVE RIGHT TO THE TREE OF LIFE, AND

MAY ENTER IN THROUGH THE GATES INTO THE CITY. Revelation, Chapter 22, Verse 14.

Without Christ we cannot enter into the Throne Room of God to find grace and help in the time of need. Grace opened the doorway to Heaven, but Christ is the door (gate) to the City. Faith in the FINISHED WORKS OF CHRIST is the KEY which opens the door to the City for all who believe. Believing what Jesus accomplished at the Cross REVERSES THE CURSE when we are trusting in His finished works.

Faith in the FINISHED WORKS OF CHRIST is all we need to find peace and rest in this World. Because Christ finished the work He was sent to earth to accomplish, we can rest in faith. WITHOUT FAITH IT IS IMPOSSIBLE TO PLEASE GOD. Therefore, if we are going to please God we must possess and maintain a measure of Faith.

THE AUTHOR AND FINISHER

WHEN JESUS THEREFORE HAD RECEIVED THE VINEGAR, HE SAID, IT IS FINISHED: AND HE BOWED HIS HEAD AND GAVE UP THE GHOST. John, Chapter 19, Verse 30. If we have Faith in the FINISHED WORKS OF CHRIST we are His chosen, His anointed, and His children.

When Jesus was dying on the Cross He said "IT IS FIN-ISHED"— which in Greek means "It is paid in full." In making this statement Jesus was confirming to a lost and dying World that the curse of sin had been transferred to Him. He, who knew no sin, had become sin in order that mankind could find Eternal Life through Faith in His sacrifice. Without faith it is IMPOSSIBLE to please God.

THEN SAID I, LO, I COME: IN THE VOLUME OF THE BOOK IT IS WRITTEN OF ME. Psalms 40, Verse 7; Hebrews, Chapter 10, Verse 7. Jesus delighted in doing the Will of His Father. God's laws were written on His Heart. Jesus came to bring spiritual sight to spiritually blinded eyes and undo what the Serpent had accomplished in the Garden of Eden.

Christ is the AUTHOR AND FINISHER OF OUR FAITH. Jesus, despising the shame but looking forward to the joy that was before Him, became the eternal Author and Finisher of our faith. He penned the very words which offer salvation to the souls of all who choose to believe In Him.

Every prophetic jot and tittle in Scripture was fulfilled by the Author Himself. Jesus dotted every "i" and crossed every "t" which was written by Him. He left no question unanswered regarding who He was and what He was sent to Earth to accomplish. The Light of Christ became our understanding. He fulfilled every letter that formed each word, and every word that completed each sentence and then sat down at the RIGHT HAND OF GOD.

MAN SHALL NOT LIVE BY BREAD ALONE, BUT BY EVERY WORD THAT PROCEEDS OUT OF THE MOUTH OF GOD. Matthew, Chapter 4, Verse 4.

Christ fulfilled every word the Ancient Scribes wrote about Him. He was the BREAD OF LIFE, as well as the TREE OF LIFE. His LIFE is the LIGHT which leads us down the PATH LEAST TRAVELED toward the Tree of Life.

Christ is the Truth, the Life and the Way. He is the Living Word. The Word became Flesh, dwelt among men, and now dwells within their hearts if they accept Him as Lord and Savior. He is the SEED OF PROMISE which bruised the head of the Serpent at Calvary.

The Word of Life (Christ) leads us down the road of life toward the Tree of Life. He is our Life, and without Him, living is in vain. Without Christ, we are nothing. In Him we become the sons and daughters of God, and God is not ashamed to call us His own.

CHRIST CAME IN THE BOOK WRITTEN OF HIM, to fulfill the Will of the Father for Him to become a Living Sacrifice for our sins. CHRIST STILL WALKS IN THE PAGES OF THE BOOK to fulfill and complete His glorious work in us. He sent His Word to heal and deliver mankind from all of their destructions. Psalms, 107, Verse 20.

When we see Christ in the VOLUME OF THE BOOK which was written of Him, we must see ourselves doing the things He did. He has given us the GREAT COMMISION to "go into the World and Preach the Gospel." Mark, Chapter 16, Verses 15-18. As we walk down the PATH LEAST TRAVELED, we must DENY OURSE-VLVES AND PICK UP OUR CROSS TO FOLLOW AFTER HIM.

When reading the VOLUME OF THE BOOK, we must find ourselves feeding the hungry, healing the sick, raising the dead, and casting out demons just as Christ did during His earthly Ministry. This also is part of the Great Commission. If we are not doing all we have been commanded to do, we are not fulfilling the HIGH CALLING OF GOD.

When we see Jesus on the Cross, we must also see our-selves hanging on the Cross with Him. Paul said, "I AM CRCUCI-FIED WITH CHRIST: NEVERTHELESS I LIVE; YET NOT I, BUT CHRIST LIVETH IN ME: AND THE LIFE THAT I NOW LIVE IN THE FLESH I LIVE BY THE FAITH OF THE SON OF GOD, WHO LOVED ME, AND GAVE HIMSELF FOR ME." Galatians, Chapter 2, Verse 20.

ALL SCRIPTURE IS GIVEN BY INSPIRATION OF GOD, AND IT IS PROFITABLE FOR DOCTRINE, AND FOR REPROOF, FOR CORRECTION, FOR INSTRUCTION IN RIGHTEOUSNESS: THAT THE MAN OF GOD MAY BE PERFECT (COMPLETE), THROUGHLY FURNISHED UNTO ALL GOOD WORKS. 2 Timothy, Chapter 3, Verses 16-17.

We find everything we need to be complete in Christ in the Word of God. His Word will thoroughly furnish us with "FRUIT THAT REMAINS," as we eat daily from the Tree of Life. The Book that was written of Him, by Him, and through Him, enables us to walk the PATH LEAST TRAVELED.

If you are struggling as you press toward the MARK OF THE HIGH CALLING OF GOD IN CHRIST, there is hope in HIS FINISHED WORKS. We are transformed into the image of Christ by the renewing of our minds, line upon line and precept upon precept in each Volume of the Book written of Him and by Him— THE BIBLE.

The scripture tells us that ALL THINGS WORK TOGETHER FOR GOOD FOR THOSE WHO LOVE GOD AND ARE CALLED ACCORDING TO HIS PURPOSE. Romans, Chapter 8 Verse 28. In whatever situation we find ourselves, we must take every opportunity to grow in Christ. If we will seek Knowledge, Wisdom and Understanding in every circumstance of life, we will find Christ anxiously waiting and willing to instruct us in Righteousness.

MAY THE PEACE OF GOD WHICH PASSES ALL UNDERSTANDING GUARD YOUR HEART AND MIND IN CHRIST JESUS. MAY GOD BLESS AND KEEP YOU SAFE IN YOUR PURSUIT OF HIM.

IF YOU DO NOT KNOW JESUS CHRIST AS YOUR LORD AND SAVIOR, OR IF YOU HAVE BACKSLIDDEN OR NOT SURE WHERE YOU SHOULD BE IN THE LORD—PLEASE PRAY THIS PRAYER AND ASK JESUS TO COME INTO YOUR HEART AND LIFE:

FATHER I COME TO YOU IN THE NAME OF YOUR SON JESUS. I ADMIT THAT I AM A SINNER AND THAT I HAVE COME SHORT OF YOUR GLORY. I BELIEVE THAT JESUS DIED ON THE CROSS FOR MY SINS AND THAT YOU RAISED HIM FROM THE DEAD. I KNOW THAT IT WAS FOR ME THAT JESUS DIED. I AM SORRY FOR ALL THE SINS I HAVE COMMITTED. PLEASE FORGIVE ME AND COME INTO MY HEART RIGHT NOW. I ALSO ASK YOU TO FILL ME WITH THE HOLY SPIRIT. AMEN.

Signature and Date:

_____

OTHER BOOKS BY DON RANDOLPH

I AM- A Prophetic Look At End Time Events

IT IS WRITTEN-Exposing The Works Of The Flesh

A MESSAGE TO THE CHURCHES

SPIRITUAL WARFARE-And the Craft Of Deception

THE NEW JERUSALEM

THE STORY OF THE CROSS

THE LAW OF LOVE

THE VAGABOND SPIRIT

A CRY IN THE WILDERNESS

THE FIRST NATIONS INITIATIVE

PROPHETIC POETRY

THE KNOWLEDGE OF GOD

THE WISDOM OF GOD

PURSUING THE DIVINE NATURE OF CHRIST

DIVNE LEADERSIP DIRECTIVES AND DISPOSITIONS

THE SPIRIT AND THE BRIDE SAY COME

EXPOSING AND DETHRONING LUCIFER

DECEPTION--THE OPIATE OF THE MASSES

UNVEILING THE MYSTERY OF EDEN

BOOT CAMP BRIDE

BOOKLETS

WHO TOLD YOU THAT YOU WERE NAKED

THE SPIRIT OF FEAR

A MESSAGE FROM THE SEVEN STARS

IN MY FATHER'S HOUSE

THE STORM

THE PATH LEAST TRAVELED

VISIONS OF RAPTURE-Poetry

THE ROSE OF SHARON-Poetry

THE WISDOM OF THE AGES-Poetry

Email address: donrandolph@gmail.com

Printed in the United States
By Bookmasters